"People don't need someone else telling them what to do and how to think—they need stimulating, 'God-led' information that enables them to draw out the leadership gifts and ideas that God has already placed within their hearts and minds. That's what *Secrets of Everyday Leaders* does— and that's why it will continue to produce fruit long after the material has been filed away."

—*Mike Hiltibidal, Everyday Leader*

"The folks at the Myers Institute are real people, not building an agenda or a bank account. They are motivated to impact the world by instilling vision into the hearts of ordinary individuals. During World War II, the enemy knew it could not defeat the United States because where a leader fell, a soldier rose and became a leader. The Myers Institute is building us soldiers into leaders."

—*Merry Hoffman, Everyday Leader*

"*Secrets of Everyday Leaders* has placed leadership training on the bottom shelf, where most of us live the day-to-day realities of life, where we can easily access and apply the profound truths inherent in effective leadership. I believe this tool will prove to shape many of the rising leaders of this generation, and the next."

—*Rich Hart, Everyday Leader*

"Saying 'Dr. Jeff Myers wrote a coaching system about leadership' is like saying 'the Chinese built a wall.' Jeff takes simple principles and weaves them into something incredible. *Secrets of Everyday Leaders* not only provides practical, understandable, usable information...it is also a huge source of inspiration. It not only tells me how to be a leader, it makes me long to be one."

—*Ed Buice, Everyday Leader*

"*Secrets of Everyday Leaders* is exactly the type of material I have been hunting for to use with the teenage co-ops that I teach. This system includes everything I had in mind: inspiration, real-life examples, biblical examples, and motivation for action. Jeff is easy and enjoyable to listen to, and he definitely has a gift for putting together materials that make it easy to inspire youth to leadership!"

—*Pat Wesolowski, Everyday Leader*

"I LOVE IT!! *Secrets of Everyday Leaders* is good stuff, Dr. Jeff! I like the way you balance personal stories, which I personally love to hear, with biblical and historical people. No matter who we are, God wants to use all of us to build the Kingdom, meet needs, and reach the lost by intelligently being able to defend our faith. *Secrets of Everyday Leaders* is presented in an easy to follow, step-by-step, timeless course that will have you saying, 'If they can do it, we can, too.'"

—*Linda Tenga, Everyday Leader*

"There is such great stuff here. *Secrets of Everyday Leaders* really spoke to my heart and need as a youth group leader. The coaching tips and self-evaluation exercises included in this book are of superb benefit. This material has a great plan to help anyone begin their own personal leadership empowerment journey and help others grow in leadership qualities."

—*Angela Priest, Everyday Leader*

"This is an investment that will help train teams and individuals alike, regardless of age. It is truly written for Everyday Folks and will be a valuable leadership resource for years to come. I've learned that we all lead, whether we recognize it or not. If we choose to develop our influence on those around us, we increase our effectiveness as we journey alongside others to help them pilot a godly, satisfying life. *Secrets of Everyday Leaders* helps this happen in practical step-by-step fashion."

—*Lynn Fote, Everyday Leader*

"Jeff has thoroughly embraced leadership and passionately passed it on. I'm grateful! *Secrets of Everyday Leaders* is practical material packaged in easy-to-understand and memorable ways. Jeff's ideas are accurate, complete, and relevant, and his use of Bible heroes and case studies is inspiring. Because he includes the 'whats,' 'whys,' and 'hows' of leadership, you'll be convinced you can and should lead, and you'll be able to! I know I'll often recommend these materials."

—*Kathy Koch, Everyday Leader*

"You would think as you hear Jeff Myers tell about his desperate fear of public speaking that he would have been a prime candidate for one 'least likely to lead and influence.' Instead, Jeff makes a conscious choice to allow God to define his potential. Jeff keeps you on the 'edge of your seat' with his dynamic style as he encourages, instructs, and inspires you to become the leader God has designed you to be."

—*Joanne Darling, Everyday Leader*

"This book targets those of us who need its encouragement most, those who are not 'leaders' in the world's eyes. As a mother with three pre-teen children, the question of how to lead my children so their hearts will follow is always before me."

—*Melanie West, Everyday Leader*

SECRETS OF
EVERYDAY LEADERS

Create Positive Change
and Inspire Extraordinary Results

SECRETS OF EVERYDAY LEADERS

Create Positive Change and Inspire Extraordinary Results

A Coaching Manual to Accompany
the Leadership Coaching System by

Jeff Myers, Ph.D.

BROADMAN
&HOLMAN
PUBLISHERS

Nashville, Tennessee

10-digit ISBN: 0805468862
13-digit ISBN: 9780805468861

Published by Broadman & Holman Publishers
Nashville, Tennessee

DEWEY: 303.3
SUBHD: LEADERSHIP

Scripture text is from The Holy Bible, *Holman Christian Standard Bible*®, Copyright © 1999, 2000, 2001, 2002, 2003
by Holman Bible Publishers. Other "Credits, Permissions, and Sources" are listed at the back of the book.

1 2 3 4 5   09 08 07 06 05

Dedicated To:

The memory of Brent Noebel
and to the Summit graduates
who are building the wall
all over the world.

CONTENTS

ACKNOWLEDGMENTS

Special thanks to:

Jerry Thorpe, Regina Thorpe, Evan Thorpe,
Wayne Smith, Meleah Smith,
Todd Cothran, Chris White, Staci Davis, Joel Putnam, Alana Toliver,
the whole Summit Ministries team,
and the students in my leadership classes at Bryan College.

INTRODUCTION

You've Been Put in Charge. Now What?

EVERYONE REACTS TO LEADERSHIP opportunities differently. And people don't necessarily make good leaders just because they *want* to lead. Very often, the reluctant leader is the one who really gets things done.

You may or may not be particularly interested in being a leader. But you do want to see things change, and you realize the only way to make it happen is to influence others.

That's what leadership is all about: *change* and *influence*. This leadership coaching system will help you influence others and change things in a way that inspires admiration, respect, creativity, and vision.

The whole point of talking about "everyday leaders" is that everyone needs to develop leadership skills for some aspect of life. That's what this book and the first six DVD sessions of the training package are all about. In lessons 1 through 6, you'll learn:

• How to lead when you're not in charge;

• The three keys to becoming credible in the eyes of your followers;

• Embracing the eloquent life: what it means to be "above reproach" and to handle your responsibilities gracefully and without excuses;

• Where to find the "Solomons"—the wise people who have the answers to every problem you'll face;

• How to be a good follower and how that can transform you into a good leader;

• Equipping followers to become tougher and more dedicated the harder things get.

Whether you're the head of a business or organization or simply fulfilling your calling as a parent or student, you'll benefit from applying the principles I've outlined. If you're currently involved in some formal leadership role, however—at church, work, school, or in government—you'll likely need even more help. That's where the advanced training on the second six DVD sessions comes in.

These lessons coach you on critical leadership activities like:

• Ways to cast a vision and to inspire your followers with excitement for your mission.

• Strategically planning your group's success;

• Banishing apathy and moving people toward higher and higher levels of commitment;

• Enlisting the gifts and skills of others to move rapidly toward your goal;

• Decisively working through the problems that all leaders face; and

• Resolving the inevitable conflicts in a way that cements followers' loyalty and creates a caring culture in your organization.

How To Get the Most Out of This Coaching System

WHATEVER YOUR SITUATION, start with the six basic lessons, and then move on as you need to. Each step in the *Secrets of Everyday Leaders* system offers a four-point learning strategy that allows you to discover and master each significant aspect of leadership in a surprisingly short period of time. Take a moment to read through this brief overview so that the outline for each step will make more sense.

1. Video coaching. Since I can't actually be there with you, I'll coach you through each step of the leadership development process using video programs taped with a "live" audience. By using the fill-in-the-blank outlines to record key points from each video coaching session, you will retain 80 to 90 percent more content than just by watching.

2. Dynamic review. These reviews highlight the key points from the video coaching session, but they are dynamic in that they answer the "Yes, but what about…" questions that are raised by the video coaching.

3. Let's talk about it. These thought-provoking questions draw your attention to the strategies you need in order to master each leadership skill.

4. Coaching tools. Each of the six chapters includes a "coaching tool" to help you apply what you are learning so as to boost your chances of succeeding as a leader.

Since our focus is on coming to understand how God wants to use you as a leader for His cause, the lessons are peppered with Scripture references. Although you may want to have your personal Bible handy as you read, you'll often find the relevant verses printed right in the text for ready reference. In most cases, I quote from the *Holman Christian Standard Bible*®. It's one of the newest English Bible translations available, and it's one that reflects the original biblical languages with remarkable accuracy and clarity. I hope these references help you clarify your own call to leadership as you reflect on God's Word.

Using this system, I guarantee you'll feel more confident, make better decisions, inspire more people, and start accomplishing your highest and best goals. So let's get started!

SECRETS OF
EVERYDAY LEADERS

**Create Positive Change
and Inspire Extraordinary Results**

VIDEO SESSION: GET READY TO LEAD

Video Session One (11 minutes)

You know you're a leader when...

• You create _____.

• You _____ others to create change.

• Leaders can be...

How Leaders make a difference

• Leaders get things _____.

• Leaders determine the _____ that an organization goes.

• Leaders make a difference in followers' _____

• Leaders make a difference in whether organizations _____ or _____.

CHAPTER ONE

Get Ready to Lead!

KEY QUOTE:
"I'm convinced that the final frontier in the battle against an increasingly secularized culture is not just to see the world from God's perspective, but to see ourselves from God's perspective."

CHAPTER AT A GLANCE

What Everyday Leaders Have to Say about Making a Difference

Video Coaching Session

- Leaders create change and influence others to change.
- Leaders make a difference by getting things started.
- Leaders determine the direction the organization goes.
- Leaders boost followers' performance.
- Leaders help the organization succeed.

Dynamic Review

- It's God's desire that you influence others and create change.
- The burning bush—and the burning desire to run away.
- God's promises to Moses: I am God; I made you; I will be with you; I will show you how to lead.
- Leadership-killers that keep you from making a difference.
- True rewards: the essence of leadership.
- Four tips to help you see yourself in a new way and embrace the challenge of leadership.

Coaching Tool

- Answer these 10 questions to determine whether or not you're called to leadership.

THIS IS NOT YOUR typical leadership book. There are lots of things missing from it—interviews with multi-billion dollar financiers or Fortune 500 CEO's, breathless stories of professional athletes and coaches. And, I dutifully report, I did not ask one U.S. Senator for his opinions on leadership. What you'll find instead are:

- Inspiring examples of everyday people who decided to make a difference...and did!
- Practical tips so you can do the same in your situation.

> "We are sent into this world to build up characters which will be blessed and useful in that great future for which we are being trained."[1]
>
> —F. B. Meyer

The Problem with Books on Leadership

Most folks don't aspire to be rich and powerful, jetting around the world to make high-powered deals. Sure, the private jet thing would be nice. So would the 5-star hotels. But that's not on the minds of most folks. What about you?

• Maybe you're a community activist. You're not as concerned with million-dollar finance deals as with what to do now that you're in charge of next year's fundraiser.

• Maybe you're a mom or dad. You probably don't have a plan to enlighten the masses—you just want to have a valuable impact on your kids.

• Maybe you're a student leader. You're not looking for an Oscar—you just want everybody to have a good time at the homecoming celebration you're helping to plan.

• Maybe you're at work, doing "business as usual." You won't be brokering any Middle East peace plans—you just want to do a good job and get people to work well together.

This book will help you—because little things make a big difference. As you seek to influence others with integrity, God will magnify your impact in the lives of others and fill you with a sense of satisfaction and significance.

Everyday leadership is a beautiful thing to see. It happens over and over every single day, all around the world. The stories of a thousand everyday heroes are written on the hearts of tens of thousands who *noticed*. And those who noticed are changed, however subtly—as a stone in a pond sends ripples across the water until millions notice, and the entire world is changed.

God Desires That You Lead

In the video I said, "Wherever great things have been done in the world, they've been done because there have been leaders who stepped outside of their comfort zone and decided to make things happen." It is God's desire that you influence others and create change.

As I said earlier, to influence others and to create change—in a nutshell—is what leadership is.

You and I are called to lead. Perhaps you find this call hard to accept. On the other hand, you may be chomping at the bit, ready to gallop.

Either way, you're on your way to an extraordinary life of fulfillment, hard work, frustration, satisfaction, heartbreak, and eternal influence. It's all part of God's plan to shape you into His image.

The whole world is parched with thirst for people who will stand up, exert influence, and create change. Accepting the call to leadership will define much of the meaning in your life. As God uses you to exercise influence and change things, you will discover the answer to the age-old question: What is the purpose of my life?

How I Know You'll Find Purpose through Leadership

That your purpose in life has to do with leadership is something I know mostly by experience. I have the opportunity to travel and speak extensively each year, giving about 200 speeches to tens of thousands of people. It's not as big a deal as it sounds (in fact, "in the flesh" I'm terrified of public speaking), but I feel compelled to bring a message of hope and redemption to the world, and this is the way God has chosen for me to do it.

Out of the 60,000 or so people each year who graciously put up with my lectures and workshops, I get to personally interact with about a thousand. I also work closely with several hundred students in a leadership training program called the Summit at Bryan College, a program I founded ten years ago. My friends and I stay in touch through a weekly leadership e-mail newsletter that has grown to about 8,000 subscribers. I also serve as Associate Professor at Bryan College in Tennessee, where each semester I coach about 30 students in leadership.

I tell you all this because I've discovered that all these folks—young, old, and in-between—have one thing in common: God has a significant purpose for their lives, and it involves influencing others and creating change. So, you're a leader by design, whether you've exercised that potential or not.

The My-Will-for-Your-Life Scroll

Unfortunately, the difficulty of figuring out *what* to do and *how* to do it is immense. If you're like me, you've probably longed for specific, step-by-step directions. I often ask my students at Bryan College, "If God handed you a scroll and said, 'Here is My specific will for your life,' would that make you happy?" As with one voice, they say, "Yes!"

As great as it sounds to receive a My-will-for-your-life scroll, the idea also makes me very nervous. Sure, it would be great to no longer worry about finding a sense of direction in life. On the other hand, I have a feeling God expects much more of me than I do of myself. I suspect that if He gave me such a scroll I'd take one look and pass out on the spot. "God, you expect me to do *what*?!?!" Maybe that's what Moses felt when he discovered that a great God is not opposed to asking His little children to do big things.

The Burning Bush

Moses was herding sheep in the wilderness when he spied a bush that was burning, but not burning up. Fascinated, he stepped closer and heard the voice of God: "Moses, take off your shoes. This is holy ground."

Barefooted, Moses listened in astonishment as God itemized a very specific plan for his life.

Wouldn't that be great, the God of the universe speaking to you *aloud* about His detailed plan for your life?

That would solve a lot of problems, wouldn't it?

Uh, no.

You see, what God had in mind for Moses was incalculably bigger than Moses could have imagined for himself. He told Moses to go to Pharaoh and ask for the release of the Israelites (Egypt's entire working class) so they could go into the desert, defeat several rival nations, and establish a paradise on earth.

Astounded, Moses asked a question that would certainly have been on my mind, had I been in his shoes (or out of his shoes): "Who am *I* that *I* should go to Pharaoh and that *I* should bring the Israelites out of Egypt?"

The Burning Desire to Run Away

I bet Moses was sorry he asked, because the Lord ratcheted up His demands a notch or two. Not only must Moses persuade the Israelite elders to let him—a sheep-herder and fugitive from justice—be their new leader, but he must also confront Pharaoh directly. Moses even received the encouraging news that Pharaoh would say "no." This would give God the opportunity to demonstrate such astounding wonders that the people of Egypt would set the Israelites free and hand over all Egypt's wealth to them on the way out.

Can you imagine what Moses must have been thinking? "Was I born yesterday? I *know* this Pharaoh—I grew up in his house. He thinks *he* is God and he *definitely* doesn't want to hear

that there's competition from You. Oh yes, and I killed one of his servants so I'm probably not on his top ten list of who he would like to spend time with today."

Moses doubted. He peppered God with questions, and God responded *again*:

"Now, Who did You say You are?"
"I Am that I Am."
"How am I to pull this off?"
"I will be with you."
"I lack self-confidence. What about that?"
"Don't you think I know that? *I made you just the way you are.*"

God didn't let Moses off the hook simply because it would be a hard job. Instead, He made four promises to Moses:

I am God.
I made you.
I will be with you.
I will show you how to lead.

Like Moses, you will find those four statements to be God's Word in your own life of leadership, too.

The Moses in Me

Moses is a terrific example of a leader because he was so...human.

For starters, Moses was an *ordinary guy*. I mean, how else can you explain his wandering around the wilderness for 40 years without stopping for directions? He owned a little sheep-herding business, had a wife and kids, and lived in the country. His life was on "cruise."

But the burning bush changed everything. Moses went from herding hundreds of *sheep* in a corner of the desert to herding millions of *people* around every square inch of desert. Along the way he had a crash course in being a diplomat, a general, a judge, and spiritual guide.

He also felt scared, inadequate. And although Moses was tapped for leadership by Almighty God (a fact confirmed through irrefutable signs and wonders), he still experienced trouble: an angry temper, rebellious followers, bothersome co-workers, too much work, and not enough time.

I'm sure Moses often called to mind what God had said, "Who made the human mouth? Who makes him mute or deaf, seeing or blind? Is it not I, the Lord? Now go! I will help you speak and I will teach you what to say." (Exodus 4:11-12)

All through his life, Moses needed to be reminded:

I am God.
I made you.
I will be with you.
I will show you how to lead.

Moses struggled against his call to leadership. He continually defined himself as a failure. And since we all face that tendency, it's worth addressing head on.

Leadership-Killers that Keep You from Really Living

Most of us are like Moses. We don't mind leading as long as it is in a time, place, and manner of our choosing—whether as a mom or dad, supervisor, business owner, or committee member. It's tough sometimes, but we have it under control—cruise control. God's plan for you, though, is likely far greater than you have in mind. His is a plan you can't just cruise through.

How do you react when I say that? Maybe you freeze up like a squirrel on the Daytona Speedway. *"What on earth am I doing here?! I'll never survive!!"* Perhaps you say, like Moses, *"Who am I to…"* But God wants to take you to a new level of living—a level where your meaning in life grows in proportion to the impact you have on others.

If you react like Moses (or the squirrel), maybe it's because you've believed one of the killer lies that leaders sometimes buy into. When left unchecked, they'll suck the life right out of you, so you'll need to know how to handle them.

Killer Lie #1: Fear

Moses thought fear would excuse him from duty. God, however, didn't see it that way.

Most people are bound up with fear in one way or another. We fear failure. We fear looking bad. We fear not knowing what to do in the tough situations we know we'll face. Some people even fear *success* because it leads to change, and change is uncomfortable. I've even seen a few clever individuals deal with their fear by casting a vision so far-fetched that they know they'll never reach it. Thus, they *appear* to be vision-driven, but they never have to make a serious effort. No matter what the disguise, though, it's still fear.

Killer Lie #2: Daydreams

A second thing that prevents true leadership is our daydreams. Daydreamers feel controlled by their environment, so they merely fantasize about an alternative reality. Daydreamers *blame* their situation on something or someone rather than seeking to transform it. They say, *"I could make a difference…"*

- "if only I could just get out of this lousy job";

- "if only I didn't live in this backwater";

- "if only I weren't surrounded by morons";

- "if only my spouse and children would support me."

The ideal leadership situation will never come along, so you'll always have an excuse. For Moses, it was his insecurity about public speaking. For Gideon, it was that he didn't come from a well-known family.

I've always been challenged by the life of evangelist David Ring. His body wracked with cerebral palsy, he moves with great pain and labors to produce words understandable to others. Yet he ministers all over America. His show-stopping line is: "I have cerebral palsy. What's your problem?"

Killer Lie #3: Inadequacy

A third leadership-killer is a feeling of inadequacy. In seventh grade, when asked what I wanted to be, I said, "a major league baseball player." Why? Because I was the worst baseball player in our town (this is no exaggeration). I thought if I could master baseball, I could gain acceptance. But since I defined myself by my inadequacy, I talked myself out of acting on my dream. In fact, I didn't even sign up for the baseball team that year.

Do you recognize the sounds of inadequacy?

- "If I can't be like so-and-so, I'm no good at all."

- "Who would listen to me?"

- "I'm just a little person in a big world."

- "I can't do that. I'm not certified."

Inadequacy allows you to bow out of responsibility with a pretense of dignity because you are claiming to be helpless. Fortunately, my parents and others who cared turned me away from my inadequacy and pointed me toward my design. Only then did the scales fall off of my eyes so I could see God's power and what He desires of me.

Killer Lie #4: Self-Imposed Limitations

What is it you think you *cannot* do? For 68 years, Walter George's 1886 record of running the mile in 4 minutes, 12.75 seconds was thought to be insurmountable. Then, Roger Bannister broke the 4-minute mark. It had been a massive case of self-imposed limitation, and amazingly, within weeks of Bannister setting the new record, John Landy and Peter Snell both broke the record as well, posting times even better than Bannister's.

Think of it: for nearly seven decades runners had bumped up against a psychological barrier—"It's not possible to beat the record, so I can't do it"—until Roger Bannister sped past it and gave the world's running community a psychological boost. How much of what you're called to do seems impossible because you've made up your mind that it is? What self-imposed barriers prevent you from achieving God's highest purposes for your life?

Killer Lie #5: Apathy

The fifth leadership-killer is apathy. The word means "without passion." While it doesn't suggest you don't care, it does signify that your horse simply doesn't have the giddy-up to go do something about whatever needs doing. Apathy says:

- "Someone else will do it."

- "I tried before and got burned."

- "It doesn't affect me that much—I can live with things the way they are."

- "Yawn. Can we leave now?"

These five leadership-killers suffocate initiative and snuff out courage. If they've got you by the throat, I have to tell you something that I myself face on a daily basis: *God doesn't need your permission to call you out into leadership.* He will consistently push you out of the nest until you begin to soar.

In his famous book *Mere Christianity*, C.S. Lewis makes the following observation:

The more we get what we now call "ourselves" out of the way and let Him take us over, the more truly ourselves we become. There is so much of Him that millions and millions of "little Christs," all different, will still be too few to express Him fully. He made them all. He invented—as an author invents characters in a novel—all the different men that you and I were intended to be. In that sense our real selves are all waiting for us in Him.[3]

Then on the next page, he delivers the real kicker:

Keep back nothing. Nothing that you have not given away will ever

Banishing fear

Here are four quick coaching tips to help you see yourself in a new way and embrace the challenge of leadership:

1. This week, pray that God will pinpoint areas of your life where you allow a fear of failure, or a fear of success, to stop you from pursuing what you know He wants you to do.

2. Study at least three Scripture heroes, such as Moses, Mary, Gideon—just about anybody—who felt inadequate, yet trusted God and succeeded.

3. Identify and write down your self-imposed limitations, pick one, and begin breaking it.

4. Thumb your nose at the consumer culture at least once each day—maybe twice. You'll notice an immediate surge of confidence when it loses its grip. You may have to toss the TV to pull this one off!

be really yours. Nothing in you that has not died will ever be raised from the dead. Look for yourself, and you will find in the long run only hatred, loneliness, despair, rage, ruin, and decay. But look for Christ and you will find Him, and with Him everything else thrown in.[4]

The life you've always wanted is before you. The lamp is waiting to be lit. Your legacy is yet to be etched in stone.

Our self-definitions are inadequate because they occur in a slice of time—the way *we* think of ourselves *right now*, rather than the way God designed us to be, full of the potential He has placed in our lives. But when we allow God to define us, amazing things happen.

Don't Look Back, the Time's Wastin'

This reality—of finding yourself in Christ and changing the world—is one that my friend, Brent Noebel, discovered a few years ago. What happened as a result changed a lot of lives and made a lasting impression on me.

I've known very few people whose life on earth was as hard as Brent's and who desired heaven so much. Yet in his battles, he inspired thousands.

Since childhood, Brent struggled with severe diabetes, kidney failure, and untold pain and suffering. Over nearly two decades, I saw Brent during good times, when the suffering ebbed a bit, and during times when it was unbearable and he wished to die. Once,

I helped Brent into a car to be rushed to the hospital, certain he would never return. Yet he did come back, time and time again.

I remember Brent describing his frustration and regret at not having lived fully for the Lord. But when he realized that time was running out, Brent got on fire. "With whatever time God gives me, I will make the biggest difference I can, for Him." At that point, Brent expected death at any moment, but for four years he handed out Gospel tracts and shared Christ with others. He dedicated his life to alleviating suffering around the world, especially among the oppressed Christians of southern Sudan in Africa.

Amazing Grace, How Sweet the Sound

Every summer morning in Colorado, Brent and his dog, Bjorn, plodded over to the Summit Ministries Leadership Camp to describe to the attending students the plight of Sudanese Christians. He always concluded his report by leading the students in the hymn "Amazing Grace." Those who heard it will never forget Brent's booming voice, "I once was lost but now am found. Was blind but now I see."

Brent challenged everyone he met to give sacrificially for items requested by the Sudanese Christians: Bibles, medical supplies, and Christian flags so they could identify themselves as soldiers of the cross.

It's curious that Brent cared about Gospel tracts, Bibles, and flags. You see, Brent was blind. He couldn't read the Bible. He couldn't see flags flying. He knew only darkness and could go only where his seeing-eye dog could take him.

Of all of Brent's infirmities, the dark world of blindness had been the hardest to bear. He once told me, "I can handle just about anything, but the darkness of the last 20 years has been sheer torture."

Brent knew what it was to persevere when there seemed to be no hope. He had faith that one day the Savior who had brought light to his soul would once again bring light to his eyes, and that this same Savior offers light and hope to oppressed people no matter where they live.

Doing What's Right When You Don't Feel Like It

During the last four years of Brent's life, while enduring excruciating pain, the dreary rigor of thrice-weekly dialysis (having all of his blood removed, cleaned and put back in), and the struggles of blindness, he led the Summit Ministries students to raise nearly $300,000 for Christians in the Sudan. When asked about this feat, Brent shrugged it off: "It just shows what one blind guy and a bunch of teenagers can do."

The last time I saw Brent, he was enjoying the antics of Summit counselors hosting a fund-raiser for Sudan. It was a Wednesday evening. On Thursday morning, Brent gave his Sudan report, led the students in "Amazing Grace,"

and was escorted to the dialysis clinic. I, in turn, gave some talks and caught a flight back home to Tennessee. When my plane landed, I received word that Brent had been gently ushered into the presence of his Savior.

My very first thought came from "Amazing Grace": "…was blind, but now I see… Hey! Brent can *see* now!" Imagine that. After having been blind for 20 years, Brent opened his eternal eyes to gaze into the loving face of his Savior.

It must have been wonderful when Brent saw Jesus face to face. I wish I could have been there. But alas, there is unfinished work here. Like Moses, and like Brent, God has called you and me to tasks we are quite certain transcend our limited abilities.

Brent knew, and now you and I know, that God doesn't call us because He knows we can do it. He calls us because:

He is God;
He made us;
He will be with us;
He will show us how to lead.

True Rewards: The Essence of Leadership

Exciting things happen once you obediently embrace the call to leadership. In fact, I'm convinced you'll never experience true fulfillment in life until you take that leap. Nevertheless, the plain fact is, leadership is *hard*. Lots of people *claim* to be leaders, but very few actually *lead*.

Leadership is also costly. Like Moses, you may be challenged beyond what you think you can bear. You might fail. You might be rejected by the very people you're trying to lead. You might lead for your whole life and never reach your destination.

I'm convinced the final frontier in the battle against an increasingly secularized culture is not just to see the *world* from God's perspective, but to see *ourselves* from God's perspective. Only then will we understand that our sovereign God works through pain and travail to provide unbelievable peace, joy, satisfaction, a sense of meaning, and a lasting influence on the world around us.

That's the leadership journey. Are you ready for another step in that direction?

Notes

1. F. B. Meyer, *F. B. Meyer: The Best from All His Works*, Charles Erlandson, ed. (Nashville: Thomas Nelson Publishers, 1988), p. 60.

2. A. W. Tozer, *The Knowledge of the Holy* (Lincoln, NE: Back to the Bible Broadcast, 1961), p. 106.

3. C. S. Lewis, *Mere Christianity* (San Francisco, CA: Harper, 2001), p. 189.

4. Ibid., p. 190.

LET'S TALK ABOUT IT:

In the video, Dr. Myers talked about the "disconnect" between what we know to be true and what we can actually do. Some have called this a "leadership gap." How have you seen it manifested? How have you seen this disconnect in your own life?

What are the areas of your life in which you have influence?

What are the things around you that need to be changed?

COACHING TOOL

Answer These 10 Questions to Determine Whether or Not You're Called to Leadership

QUESTIONS	YES	NO
Do you believe that Almighty God is the Lord of the Universe? (Psalm 100:3)		
Has God given you gifts that could be used to influence others? (1 Corinthians 12:4-11)		
Do you see anything in the world that needs to be changed? (Colossians 3:23)		
Have there been people in your life whose encouragement has helped you live a better life? (Hebrews 10:24)		
Do you feel a sense of responsibility to pay it forward by having a positive influence on others? (2 Timothy 2:2)		
Do you believe in the creation mandate that we are to be fruitful with our gifts by exercising our influence? (Genesis 1:28)		
Do you believe in the Great Commission Section's call to disciple and to teach all nations of the earth? (Matthew 28:18-20)		
Do you believe that God cares for you and guides you? (Philippians 4:6-7)		
Do you believe that God's principles can give you guidance as you learn to lead? (Joshua 1:9)		

Scoring (number of "Yes" answers):

8–10 Get ready to lead!

4–7 Study the Scripture verses next to each question and retake the test.

1–3 Check to see if you have a pulse!

SCRIPTURE REFERENCES FOR CHAPTER ONE COACHING TOOL

Review These Scriptures to Affirm God's Call to Leadership

Psalm 100:3—Acknowledge that the Lord is God. He made us, and we are His—His people, the sheep of His pasture.

1 Corinthians 12:4-11—Now there are different gifts, but the same Spirit. [5]There are different ministries, but the same Lord. [6]And there are different activities, but the same God is active in everyone and everything. [7]A manifestation of the Spirit is given to each person to produce what is beneficial: [8]to one is given a message of wisdom through the Spirit, to another, a message of knowledge by the same Spirit, [9]to another, faith by the same Spirit, to another, gifts of healing by the one Spirit, [10]to another, the performing of miracles, to another, prophecy, to another, distinguishing between spirits, to another, different kinds of languages, to another, interpretation of languages. [11]But one and the same Spirit is active in all these, distributing to each one as He wills.

Colossians 3:23—Whatever you do, do it enthusiastically, as something done for the Lord and not for men.

Hebrews 10:24—And let us be concerned about one another in order to promote love and good works.

2 Timothy 2:2—And what you have heard from me in the presence of many witnesses, commit to faithful men who will be able to teach others also.

Genesis 1:28—God blessed them [Adam and Eve], and God said to them, "Be fruitful, multiply, fill the earth, and subdue it. Rule the fish of the sea, the birds of the sky, and every creature that crawls on the earth."

Matthew 28:18-20—Then Jesus came near and said to them, "All authority has been given to Me in heaven and on earth. [19]Go, therefore, and make disciples of all nations, baptizing them in the name of the Father and of the Son and of the Holy Spirit, [20]teaching them to observe everything I have commanded you. And remember, I am with you always, to the end of the age."

Philippians 4:6-7—Don't worry about anything, but in everything, through prayer and petition with thanksgiving, let your requests be made known to God. [7]And the peace of God, which surpasses every thought, will guard your hearts and your minds in Christ Jesus.

Joshua 1:9—"Haven't I commanded you: be strong and courageous? Do not be afraid or discouraged, for the Lord your God is with you wherever you go."

VIDEO SESSION: HOW TO GET OTHERS TO TAKE YOU SERIOUSLY

Video Session Two (18 minutes)

Getting Others to Take You Seriously

- Are you _____? Do potential followers believe you will be a good leader?

- Are you _____? Can potential followers be sure you will treat them with dignity and integrity?

- Are you _____? Are you capable of going to bat for what is really important?

CHAPTER TWO

How to Get Others to Take You Seriously

KEY QUOTE:

"Credibility is the foundation of leadership."

CHAPTER AT A GLANCE

Gaining Credibility as a Leader

Video Coaching Session Summary
• Why credibility is important to leadership.
• How to establish that you know what you're doing.
• What makes followers trust or distrust you.
• How to be dynamic—it's not what you think!

Dynamic Review
• What makes others want to listen and believe?
• Credibility is the foundation of leadership.
• The three questions your followers are asking.
• Knowing what you're doing without knowing everything.
• Trustworthiness: being a person of admirable character.
• Four strategies for gaining followers' trust.
• The dynamo in you: how to take charge and get things done.
• Getting things done: a case study.
• Winning life-long loyalty.
• Share the love: viral encouragement.
• Listen up! A simple way to show you care.

Coaching Tool
How credible are you? This assessment reveals your credibility strengths and weaknesses.

PEOPLE WILL ONLY FOLLOW you if they see you as credible and trustworthy. This is true whether you manage others at work, exert influence in a church or social organization, or raise children.

Just because you have a position of authority does not mean others accept your leadership. Once you establish yourself as a leader worth following, others will respond more enthusiastically to your leadership and become more deeply committed to reaching your organization's goals.

So how can you gain credibility? That's what this chapter is all about. You'll discover how to show followers that you know what you're doing, you'll find authentic ways to gain the trust of those you lead, and you'll learn techniques for becoming a more dynamic leader.

Familiarity's Breeding Program

One morning I approached my office at Bryan College with a spirit of dread, having faced a particularly rambunctious and frustrating group of students the day before. I couldn't help but smile, though, when I found a repentant undergraduate's conciliatory paraphrase of Scripture taped to my office door:

The Sermon on the Mount (Teacher Edition)

Then Jesus took His disciples up on the mountain and gathering them around Him, He taught them, saying:

Blessed are the poor in spirit for theirs is the kingdom of heaven.

Blessed are the meek.

Blessed are they that mourn.

Blessed are they who thirst for justice.

Blessed are you when persecuted.

Blessed are you when you suffer.

Be glad and rejoice, for your reward is great in heaven.

Then Simon Peter said, 'Do we have to write this down?'

And Andrew said, 'Are we supposed to know this?'

And James said, 'Will we have a test on it?'

And Phillip said, 'What if we don't know it?'

And Bartholomew said, 'Do we have to turn this in?'

And John said, 'The other disciples didn't have to learn this.'

And Matthew said, 'When do we get out of here?'

And Judas said, 'What does this have to do with real life?'

Then one of the Pharisees present asked to see Jesus' lesson plans and inquired as to His terminal objectives in the cognitive domain.

And Jesus wept.

In any situation, credibility is hard to get—a fact I can relate to as a teacher, a parent, a boss, a neighbor, and a church member—and it is hardest to get from those who know you. As the saying goes, "Familiarity breeds contempt."

But what makes someone worth following even after you get to know that person? Let's outline some answers to that question.

Are You Worth Following?

What is credibility anyway? The word comes from the Latin "credo," which means, "to have faith or trust in." To have credibility means you can be trusted because you're a person of character who knows how to get things done.

Credibility comes down to this: Is what you believe worth following? In their book, *Credibility*, James Kouzes and Barry Posner note:

> Above all else, people want leaders who are credible. We want to believe in our leaders. We want to have faith and confidence in them as people. We want to believe that their word can be trusted, that they have the knowledge and skill to lead, and that they are personally excited and enthusiastic about the directions in which we are headed. Credibility is the foundation of leadership.[1]

Credibility is the foundation of leadership. Those who have it climb confidently toward the summit of leadership success. Those who don't just…wander around.

Credibility has been studied for several millennia by the world's most famous philosophers. As we discussed in the video coaching lesson, Aristotle explained that there are three kinds of credibility. Let's review the list and then take a look at each in more detail, figuring out how to apply it in real life.

The Three Questions Your Followers Are Asking

You can't buy credibility or force others to give it to you. You can only get it the old-fashioned way: *earn* it. As I showed in the video coaching lesson,

your followers and peers assess your credibility by seeking answers to three profoundly simple questions. Answer these questions authoritatively, and you'll be rewarded with loyalty, hard work, and a team spirit.

Did you catch the full impact of that? You are being silently and perhaps unconsciously evaluated by those you lead. They're sizing you up, trying to decide whether to follow you and how much energy to dedicate to your cause. Basically, what they want to know is:

(1) Are you competent?

Do you know what you're doing? Perhaps you've had the experience of following a leader who didn't. It's a sinking feeling to know the person in whose wake you are swimming is barely afloat. We all shy away from such people because we're afraid of being dragged down with them! Good leaders are seen as competent not just because they know what they know, but because they know what they *don't* know—and they turn to others for help.

(2) Are you trustworthy?

Are you a good person? Do you strive to be a person of admirable character? Can people be sure you will treat them with dignity and respect? Self-centered leaders raise suspicion. When they express interest in us, we ask, "What do they want from me now?" Even when they do something nice,

> "Life, like war, is a series of mistakes, and... he is the best who wins the most splendid victories by the retrieval of mistakes."[3]
>
> —Frederick W. Robertson

we're wondering about their motives. On the other hand, leaders who live out their principles inspire our trust. They're not perfect, but we can accept their imperfections because we know they are headed in the right direction.

(3) Are you dynamic?

Do you inspire confidence? Are you willing to go to bat for what really matters? Can you get things done? Your followers' level of confidence, attitude, and determination will mirror your own. If you are bold, positive, and willing to work hard, others will catch your vision. Success breeds interest, and interest breeds action.

Now, let's lift the lid on each of these principles—competence, trustworthiness, and dynamism—so we can figure out how they work and how they might be applied to everyday leadership.

Competence: Do You Know What You're Talking About?

Michaela rolled her eyes at the boss's instructions. This place was like a living Dilbert™ cartoon! How could he expect her to develop a marketing plan and prepare her annual budget, all in the same week?

Fuming as she marched back to her cubicle, Michaela encountered her co-worker, Damon. "Wait 'til you hear what the boss just asked me to pull off this week! He thinks I can produce a new marketing plan *and* finish the budget—all during the busiest season of the year!"

"But you, my friend, are a certifiable marketing genius. You can do it! You go, girl!" Damon said, doing the cheerleader imitation Michaela usually found hilarious.

Michaela ignored him and plowed on. "Maybe it's easy for MISTER-I-CAN-WRITE-A-BUSINESS-PLAN-IN-MY-SLEEP," she said. "But I don't have any idea what I'm doing!"

"Apparently the guy has no idea what it takes to produce a marketing plan," said Damon, more soberly this time. He sighed, "We've never done it in less than two weeks of full-time work. Well, until *now*."

Michaela rolled her eyes. "Yeah, thanks for the oh-so-timely reminder. I guess I'll just do my best—I don't want him to think I can't keep up."

The Boss Is in Trouble!

Unless he learns from his employees' expertise, Michaela's boss will end up with bitter, half-hearted workers. Michaela is in trouble, too. She's determined to succeed, but she'll probably get burned out and spread discontentment to her fellow employees.

The boss is not ignorant. He is quite good at accounting and budgeting, and everyone knows it. But he demonstrates incompetence by communicating expectations without support, failing to get reasoned feedback, and underestimating the complexity of others' jobs. Michaela, in turn, fails to share from her expertise and communicate her thoughts in a forthright and respectful way. She hides her frustration from the boss, but because she's doomed to fail, Michaela is only postponing the inevitable conflict.

In the short term, this boss might lose credibility and foster sour, resistant employees. He'll probably weather that okay. In the long run, however, he will find it extremely difficult to keep good employees on his team, and the quality of work will suffer tremendously.

Knowing What You're Doing Without Knowing Everything

Your followers want to know that you know what you're doing (and so does your supervisor). Years ago I worked for a gruff but lovable boss who regularly asked, as my team was careening toward its goals, "Do we know what we're doing, Tiger?" He needed assurance that we could actually pull off our plans. His level of trust varied significantly depending on whether or not we could demonstrate success.

Perhaps you're saying, "But Jeff, that's just the problem. I *don't* know what I'm doing! How can I show that I'm competent when I'm treading water like everyone else?"

Interestingly enough, effective leaders aren't effective because they possess all the information they need. They're effective because they know how to draw on the skills and experience of others. They ask for help in learning the processes and skills they need to succeed.

Asking for help may seem counter-intuitive. After all, if you're the boss, aren't you expected to know everything? Not at all. J. J. Gabarro, a business researcher, studied individuals who successfully "take charge" of organizations. He found that they typically spend three to six months absorbing information, learning, and evaluating situations, and four to eleven months immersing themselves in day-to-day operations and developing an understanding of the organization.[2]

Did you catch that? These successful leaders spend *from seven months to one and one-half years* just seeking to understand! Of course, they don't just *learn* during this time. They act to correct short-term problems, become proficient at the process and produce a plan for improving the organization. *But the focus is on learning.*

Will asking for help lower your status with followers? It depends. You certainly don't want to appear helpless or apologetic. To get what you need, say something like, "To be more effective in my position I really need to have a better understanding of 'X.' I have heard that you are great at it. Could you show me some of the 'tricks of the trade'?"

Your followers are gifted. Being a good steward of *their* gifts as well as your own shows them you know what you're doing. It also builds their respect for you while enhancing their future leadership potential.

Share the Love

Want to make your credibility grow? Extend unlimited credit to others for doing a good job. When someone compliments you, say, "Thanks for noticing. You know, we wouldn't have been successful without the initiative and skill of [name of a person or group]. Would you make it a point to say thank you to them as well?" This kind of encouragement becomes contagious, spreading through the organization.

Winning Lifelong Loyalty

FOR MY MONEY, the single best way to win lifelong loyalty is to invest in the lives of your followers so they increase their competence! Let's say one of those on your team—Jarend—is competent as an event coordinator, but when called on to give presentations, his naturally buoyant personality goes flat. You could look for someone else to take his position, but then you'd have to start from scratch in training the new person. Plus, the new person will bring his own set of strengths and weaknesses. It's almost always better for you, the organization, and the people on your team to invest your time and energy in improving the skills of those on the team.

With Jarend you could express appreciation for the things he does well and say, "To succeed in the long-run in this job you'll need to pursue excellence in public speaking. I know you don't see yourself as a natural public speaker, but I can envision the day when you 'wow' people with your presentations. I've arranged for you to attend a course on public speaking and to meet with an expert who will help you refine and practice your presentation skills. Others who've studied with her have experienced dramatic improvement in their skill and confidence."

You can also "coach" Jarend by helping work through his presentation yourself, by encouraging him along the way, and by sharing tips that you pick up. Photocopy and give him a magazine article on presentation skills. Buy a book on sales presentations. Let him know where he can find free ideas and presentation software on-line.

Is there a point at which it is no longer worth it to go to all this effort? Yes. People who show themselves to be unteachable or unwilling to improve need to be reassigned or "given the freedom to find their success in another organization" (a nice way of saying, "fired").

Most people, however, want to do a better job, both for their own self worth and to be a better member of the team. Investing in someone wins lifelong loyalty. Here's a good maxim to live by: "Criticize a person's work, and you criticize the person's worth. Train a person to improve his work, and you improve his worth."

How Michaela's Boss Could Show Competence

Let's go back to the example of Michaela's boss. What could have happened differently if Michaela or her boss had understood these principles?

Michaela's boss could have demonstrated his competence by helping her with her struggles (developing a budget) while asking her to teach him about the process of assembling a marketing plan.

Michaela could have helped herself and her boss by requesting assistance in learning the budgeting process and by offering to explain the marketing task she faced. She could have said, "I have learned a successful formula for developing a marketing plan. May I show it to you and get your feedback?"

Build your skills and those of your followers, and you'll find that they will begin to trust your competence. But they also need to trust you as a person, and that's what we'll talk about next.

Trustworthiness: Being a Person of Admirable Character

Trust happens when people believe you'll do the right thing for the right reasons. Your followers want to know that you have the integrity to place the vision of the organization above your own personal interests and that you'll enable them to contribute to the organization's success.

Confederate General Thomas "Stonewall" Jackson was perhaps the most admired general in the Civil

A glimpse into his everyday life helps explain. Just a few months before his death, Jackson spent the winter with his officers on the estate of Mrs. Corbin in Chancellorsville, Virginia. Knowing the conditions that his troops would be staying in, Jackson refused Mrs. Corbin's invitation to use her home as his headquarters, choosing instead a one-room hunting lodge.

There in that hunting lodge, Jackson finally took the time to write up the reports of his campaigns. He worked day and night on the task. Biographer Allan Tate describes Jackson's unassuming humility:

> He never said "I"; he always said "we". . . he credited nothing to himself. "The men who come after me must act for themselves; and as to the historians who speak of the movements of my command, I do not concern myself greatly as to what they may say."[4]

Stonewall Jackson didn't consider himself a better man than his soldiers. He put the interests of his army above his own desire for accolades. As a result, Jackson garnered tremendous loyalty from his troops and officers and was successful in battle.

Five Strategies for Gaining Followers' Trust

When I conduct corporate seminars I often ask, "Can you tell the difference between a supervisor who really cares and one who just pretends to care?"

> "There is only one way under high heaven to get anybody to do anything.... And that is by making the other person want to do it."[6]
>
> —Dale Carnegie

The answers are immediate, specific, and often sarcastic. Why? Because we've all met people who want to climb their way to the top on the backs of others, and we resent it.

On the other hand, we're inspired by leaders who live out their principles and honor others. We know they're not perfect, but we forgive their imperfections because we know they're the genuine article.

What steps can you take to show your followers you're the real deal and worthy of trust in a leadership position?

(1) Always be honest. Your followers will trust you more if they know you are not "hiding" anything from them. Those in your group need communication. They need to know how you view their performance and how the organization is doing in reaching its goals. Leaders who are distracted, vague, or uncommunicative cultivate followers who are half-hearted, sloppy and unconcerned. "Why should I give my best when it doesn't seem to help and isn't even noticed?" Fortunately, it's not as hard to address this as you might think. Here's how:

- **Be open.** If there's a reason you can't give someone your full attention, say, "I'm sorry I'm distracted right now. Is there a time later today when we can talk?"

- **Be descriptive.** Don't just say, "We're working on it." Explain what you're doing to address the situation.

- **Cast a vision.** "Here's where we're headed, here are the obstacles in our way, here's why I'm confident we can succeed, and here's why you are important to this mission."

(2) Coach your followers toward success. A friend of mine who was the superintendent of a school district had a principal who did not get along well with others. My friend confronted him by saying, "If it is all right with you, I'd like to give you some feedback on your work. Here are the areas in which you're doing great, and here are some areas in which I would like to coach you if you are open to it." That principal had simply been unaware of how his behavior affected others, and he responded immediately to the feedback.

(3) Practice what you preach. Dick Wynn, former head of Youth for Christ International, spoke to my leadership class at Bryan College. During his talk, he said, "I gain credibility with my employees through the fact that I never ask them to do something that I have not done or am not willing to do."

(4) Take responsibility. Responsibility is vital, whether you're a leader or follower. Let's say you mess up something in your job, and your supervisor is furious. Instead of angering him further by making excuses, say, "I can see that what I did is extremely upsetting and that it has damaged your credibility with your superiors. I want to take full responsibility for making sure this never happens again. What specific steps should I take next time to ensure that the outcome is what you desire it to be?"

(5) Give feedback. Do your followers know you appreciate their feedback and want to hear their concerns? At the conclusion of a corporate training seminar, a man told me his supervisor habitually asked for input but never acted on it. As a result, employees stopped offering suggestions. How sad! That supervisor missed out on some potentially great ideas because he refused to offer a few seconds of feedback. Even saying, "I ran your idea by the 'higher ups,' and they want to take time to think it through," would have helped. It would have at least shown that he cared.

As you demonstrate character and caring, your credibility stock will rise. The icing on the cake, however, is that people will come to perceive you as having the energy to pull it all off. Let's dive in and see if we can plumb the depths of this important credibility booster.

The Dynamo in You: How to Take Charge and Get Things Done

The third aspect of credibility is "dynamism." Dynamic people prove to their followers they can go to bat for what is really important.

Hard Work

Some time ago, I hired several college students to help landscape our house. I assumed they were unaccustomed to difficult physical labor, so I set the pace by working as hard and as fast as I could. I moved from project to project to pitch in, to relieve someone, or to give praise. After eight hours of back-breaking work, the students were reluctant to go home. My willingness to lead dynamically set an example of enthusiasm and high performance.

Clout

"Clout" means you have credibility with *your* leaders. The evidence of the business world proves that when a boss has the ability to get the tools and resources the team needs to succeed, employees are more confident and productive. Studies of workplace satisfaction show that employees who work for supervisors with "clout" are much more satisfied and productive than those who work for powerless supervisors.

In short, if your followers know you have the actual power to influence *your* supervisors, they feel more secure that they won't end up at a deadend by following you. We'll dig into that point in greater detail in Chapter 5 when talking about how to be a good follower. In the meantime, let's look at a specific example of how dynamism elevates leadership.

Listen Up! A Simple Way to Show You Care

In their heart of hearts, people want to know that what they think matters. Leaders who listen well are more respected and more in tune with what is happening in their organizations, whether good or bad. Here are four steps to show that you're really listening:

1. Avoid outside distractions, and focus on eye contact, posture, and feedback.

2. Reflect back what the person says to you by rephrasing what they have said and asking for clarification.

3. Ask questions. Even if you understand the person perfectly well, asking a question is really the only way to "prove" that you've listened.

4. Seek first to understand, then to be understood. Gain trust by making sure you fully understand where the other person is coming from before you explain your own position.

People Follow Those Who Get Things Done: A Case Study

Douglas Hyde was a former Communist who became disillusioned with Communism but saw incredible value in the way Communist leaders in free countries inspire dedication in their followers. He wrote about his experiences in a fascinating little book called *Dedication and Leadership*.

The principles from that book form the basis of Chapter 6 in this volume, but I want to relate one of Hyde's stories here because it reveals a subtle technique for gaining credibility by focusing on the needs of others.

During World War II, Great Britain experienced a heating fuel crisis. It was bitterly cold, and people were becoming upset about living in unheated homes. Communism thrives by fanning the flames of discontent, so Communist leaders in England decided to use the fuel crisis to kick off a campaign of agitation (playing on people's dissatisfaction to get them to rebel). Hyde printed and distributed 10,000 leaflets declaring that the people refuse to "shiver in silence" and calling for action.

I'll let Hyde tell the rest of the story:

The leaflet ended by calling on housewives to go to the town hall on Thursday afternoon at 3 o'clock and make their anger known. We had practically no housewives in the Party branch and so could have no idea what the response would be.... The most we dared hope for was that sufficient people would come along...five genuine working-class housewives and Douglas Hyde...

There was, in fact, no question of getting some small deputation elected from those who were there. Thousands of angry housewives had come along to let the world know that they were not prepared to shiver in silence.

I have been in civil wars, I have been in revolutions, but I have never seen anything more frightening than thousands of angry housewives demanding fuel to warm their shivering children. They stormed the town hall; they chased the Mayor out of his parlor, then went off to the fuel office and did the same thing with the fuel officer![5]

Needless to say, the angry housewives got their fuel. And Hyde gained significant credibility with them because he showed concern and went to bat for them. Even if you're not trying to agitate people to join the Communist Party (I hope you're not!), the principle remains. By demonstrating that he could take effective action, Hyde showed his dynamism and developed immense credibility. You can do the same.

Big Stick, Soft Voice

It's important to stress that "dynamism" does not mean being loud or pushy. Teddy Roosevelt phrased it well: "Speak softly and carry a big stick." Act consistently—do what you say—and you'll develop credibility. Unfortunately, many people try to cut this process short by selfishly manipulating others. Favorite manipulation techniques include:

• Intimidating followers into complying;

• Threatening followers with harm; and

• Tricking followers into doing things that would help you but hurt them.

Manipulation may work in the short term, but ultimately it will fail. An old saying goes like this, "A man convinced against his will is a man who remains unconvinced, still." Patiently develop credibility, and you'll never have to raise your voice to accomplish your goals.

And Now It Starts

Effective leaders focus on earning credibility with their followers. They gain this trust by showing they know what they're talking about, by treating others with dignity and respect, and by demonstrating they can go to bat for things that really matter. Not only is this a godly way to treat others, but it is also the most effective way to reach your organization's goals.

Incidentally, credibility is merely one aspect of the well-lived life the Apostle Paul calls "above reproach" (1 Timothy 3:2).

Living above reproach is the critical next step in developing yourself as a leader. And that's precisely the issue we tackle in Chapter 3.

Notes

1. Kouzes & Posner *Credibility*, (San Fransisco: Jossey-Bass, 2003), p. 22.

2. John J. Gabarro *The Dynamics of Taking Charge* (Cambridge, MA: Harvard Business School Press, 1987), p. 20.

3. Frederick W. Robertson, *Sermons Preached at Brighton*, (New York: Harper and Brothers [no date of publication listed]), p. 66.

4. Allen Tate, *Stonewall Jackson: The Good Soldier* (Nashville: J.S. Sanders & Co., 1956), p. 277.

5. Douglas Hyde, *Dedication & Leadership*, (South Bend, IN: University of Notre Dame Press, 1966), p. 119.

6. Dale Carnegie, quoted in Frank Bettger, *How I Raised Myself from Failure to Success in Selling* (Englewood Cliffs, NJ: Prentice-Hall, 1949), p. 48.

LET'S TALK ABOUT IT

Take a few minutes right now and list three leaders you have observed who have great credibility. What sets them apart?

1.

2.

3.

List three areas of your life in which you would like to have greater credibility.

1.

2.

3.

(continued on next page)

(continued from previous page)

Dr. Myers explained in the video that credible leaders "know what they are talking about." Make a list of at least 5 topics you need to know about in order to become more credible as a leader (for example: conversation skill, conflict resolution, public speaking, organization, time management, etc.). Who can you turn to for help in developing those skills?

In the video coaching lesson, Dr. Myers said, "Never passively accept what is in your power to change." List two things in your life you are passively accepting right now that need to be changed.

COACHING TOOL

How credible are you?

The following exercise will help you honestly assess how credible you are in the three key areas discussed in this chapter and the video.

You will find below 13 word pairs, such as "Experienced/Inexperienced." Place an "X" at the point on each line that indicates which word best describes you in relationship to the main leadership role in your life. For example, if you feel that you are somewhat experienced, then place the "X" right in the middle, as follows:

Experienced _ _ _ x _ _ _   Inexperienced

If you believe you are very experienced, then place the "X" on the line closest to that word, and so on, until you have evaluated your credibility on all 13 word pairs.

Am I competent? Do potential followers believe I will be a good leader?

Experienced	_ _ _ _ _ _	Inexperienced
Informed	_ _ _ _ _ _	Uninformed
Skilled	_ _ _ _ _ _	Unskilled
Expert	_ _ _ _ _ _	Inexpert
Trained	_ _ _ _ _ _	Untrained

Am I trustworthy? Can potential followers be sure I will treat them with dignity and integrity?

Kind	_ _ _ _ _ _	Cruel
Friendly	_ _ _ _ _ _	Unfriendly
Honest	_ _ _ _ _ _	Dishonest
Sympathetic	_ _ _ _ _ _	Unsympathetic

Am I dynamic? Am I capable of going to bat for what is really important?

Aggressive	_ _ _ _ _ _	Hesitant
Responsive	_ _ _ _ _ _	Sheepish
Bold	_ _ _ _ _ _	Timid
Active	_ _ _ _ _ _	Passive

(Designed by communication scholars Berlo, Lemert & Mertz, 1969, and McCroskey and Young, 1983)

VIDEO SESSION: LEADING BY EXAMPLE

Video Session Three (22 minutes)

1 Timothy 3:2 — "Now the overseer must be above reproach…"

What It Means to Be above Reproach

- God does NOT expect leaders to be…

  - _____

  - _____

  - _____

- God DOES expect leaders to…

- Consistently _____ behaviors that allow followers

to _____ wrong-doing.

- Use their gifts to serve, rather than to be served.

- Lead mostly by example.

The Power of a Leader's Words

- A lesson from Gideon: encouraging words _____ his view of

his leadership potential.

- A lesson from Esther: encouraging words gave her _____ and

_____ in an impossible situation.

- A lesson from Zacchaeus: encouraging words called him out of

an _____ life.

CHAPTER THREE

Leading by Example

KEY QUOTE

"Esteem is achieved by painting the canvas of your life in the rich colors of honesty, humility, and caring, with the bold brush strokes of integrity."

CHAPTER AT A GLANCE

The Power of a Well-Lived Life

Video Coaching Session Summary
- What it means to be above reproach.
- What God expects of leaders and what He does <u>not</u> expect of them.
- The power of a leader's words—examples from Gideon, Esther, and Zacchaeus.

Dynamic Review
- What it means to be esteemed by others.
- Everything you do affects your leadership.
- Five commitments of the respected leader.
- The importance of a good reputation.
- How to graciously accept reproof.
- Would you like that lesson easy or hard?—how I learned to accept reproof.
- A leader's scars: When leadership hurts.
- The price of greatness is responsibility.
- Our lives, our fortunes, and our sacred honor.
- Making a good first impression.
- How to restore a damaged reputation.

Coaching Tool
- Discover how to build a good reputation and restore a damaged one.

As a young man of 23, Abraham Lincoln said, "Every man is said to have his peculiar ambition… I have no other so great as that of being truly esteemed by my fellow men, by rendering myself worthy of their esteem."

In Chapter 2, you learned how to gain credibility by demonstrating competence, character, and caring. There's no surer way to gain trust than to live the kind of life that demonstrates trustworthiness, and there's no surer way to self-destruct as a leader than by acting in a way that brings reproach to yourself and those you love. That's why the Apostle Paul, in addressing the qualities needed to lead churches, says, "An overseer, therefore, must be above reproach" (1 Timothy 3:2).

Does being "above reproach" mean God expects us to be sinless, well-rounded, or charismatic? I don't think so. Rather, as we discussed in the video coaching session, it means leaders must consistently avoid behaviors that allow followers to justify wrongdoing.

Everything You Do Affects Your Leadership

A popular philosophy of our day says, "It's my life. I'll live however I want." Or, "A person's private life has nothing to do with how he leads." This has not always been the sentiment, however. In 1815, the Pennsylvania Supreme Court punished six young men who had brought teenagers into a home to look at a lewd painting. The defendants argued that it was a private home and that the courts had no business interfering. But the presiding judge wrote in his opinion:

> This court is…invested with power to punish not only open violations of decency and morality, but also whatever secretly tends to undermine the principles of society… Crimes are public offenses, not because they are perpetrated publicly, but because their effect is to injure the public.[1]

As a leader, even things you do in secret have a very public effect. They affect your conscience, your ability to stand for what is right, and your ability to call your followers to a higher standard.

God wants His leaders to lead primarily by example. In this chapter, we'll expand on the lessons in the video coaching session by examining what God's kind of leader looks like, how to accept reproof, and why it's important to be above reproach even when it's costly.

Five Commitments of the Respected Leader

In the video coaching system, we discussed how to live above reproach by avoiding behaviors that set a bad example, by using God-given gifts to serve rather than to be served, and through leading mostly by example. Few biblical leaders demonstrate how to live this out better than Queen Esther.

Esther was Jewish, probably a teenager, and living as part of an ethnic and religious minority in Persia during the reign of King Xerxes. Her parents had died, so she was under the care of her relative, Mordecai, one of the king's guards, when she was chosen to be Xerxes' new queen.

About that same time, Mordecai was alerted to a plot hatched by Haman, one of the king's advisors, to kill all of the Jews in Persia. Mordecai sent a message instructing Esther to appeal to the king to change his mind. Esther wanted to help, but she recognized that appearing before the king without

Making a Good First Impression

A person's esteem for you begins with the very first encounter: "First impressions are lasting impressions." Here is a technique for making a positive first impression in a way that reflects integrity of heart. Just remember the acronym **F. I. R. S. T.**

• **F = Focus on the other person.** Leaders ask, "What can I do for this person?" Maintain a genuine interest in the other person, and you will appear "confidently humble" rather than arrogant.

• **I = Inquire about their interests.** Find out what the other person cares about. Ask questions about the "four H's": hopes, heroes, hobbies, and heart.

• **R = Remember that they are made in God's image.** Regardless of your impression of others, they are created in God's image and have inestimable value. Treat them that way.

• **S = Smile.** A smile brightens your whole countenance and warms the hearts
of others.

• **T = Tell about yourself.** Only as a last step should you talk about what interests you. As you do, seek to relate it to their interests and always end the conversation with words of encouragement.

> "What is it, Queen Esther?" the king asked her. "Whatever you want, even to half the kingdom, will be given to you."
>
> —Esther 5:3

being summoned carried the sentence of death. She must have been terrified and bewildered.

But Mordecai said, "If you keep silent at this time, liberation and deliverance will come to the Jewish people from another place, but you and your father's house will be destroyed. Who knows, perhaps you have come to the kingdom for such a time as this?" (Esther 4:14).

Though she knew it might cost her life, Esther found new reservoirs of strength and replied, "I will go to the king even if it is against the law. If I perish, I perish." Esther set her mind to appeal to the king and ultimately persuaded him through her example of graciousness and forthrightness.

Esther made five commitments that can inspire leaders today to live above reproach:

(1) Esther was *responsible.* She did not shrink from her task but accepted it even though it could cost her life. Dag Hammarskjold, a Swedish statesman who was the Secretary General of the United Nations in the 1950s, said, "To let oneself be bound by a duty from the moment you see it approaching is part of the integrity that alone justifies responsibility." God honors our fulfilling of commitments. In the parable of the minas in Luke 19, the master told the faithful servant that because he had been faithful in investing his mina, he would be given charge over ten cities.

(2) Esther was *respectful.* The Bible says Esther found favor among those in the king's court. She was gracious, likeable, and responsive to the needs of others. She didn't just "turn it on" when the situation favored her or when important people were around. Being honorable all the time is the very idea of honor. It requires holding reputation above all else no matter who is watching or who cares.

(3) Esther *represented* the king's interests. Rather than focusing on her own needs, she appealed to Xerxes based on what was important to *him*, alerting him to Haman's dangerous disloyalty. Esther understood that the king valued things that ensured his power, and she appealed to his desire for security, sovereignty, and reputation. In essence, Esther gave the king the information he needed to persuade himself.

(4) Esther *regarded* truth more highly than her own comfort. She was willing to die for her convictions, demonstrating that *success* is not as important as *obedience*. Esther could not have known she would be successful when she started, and that's the mark of a true leader: doing the right thing even if it might fail or people won't understand.

(5) Esther was *restrained.* No hard sell. No manipulation. Her cause was just, and she represented it truthfully. In this, Esther is a superb example of

a leader. She didn't get to choose the time or place in which to lead. It was an impossible situation, but she led anyway. This principle must be underscored in our own age: often people feel they can't really lead until their external circumstances improve. True leadership blossoms when there are real limits that must be taken into account. Esther couldn't go to the king without being invited, so she had to be creative. In the end, she asked the king to come to *her* for a special dinner. She must have been an amazing hostess. The king was so impressed that he offered her anything she wanted, up to half his kingdom.

Perhaps the most striking thing about Esther's story is the effect of her good reputation and kindness. Esther 2:15 says she "won approval in the sight of everyone who saw her."

The Importance of a Good Reputation

Some leaders mistakenly believe it is only important to have a good reputation in the eyes of those whose decisions will affect their future. Once, at a speaking engagement, I had an unexpected opportunity to see clearly just how wrong this opinion is.

The conference organizers had arranged for all the speeches to be taped and made available for purchase by conference attendees. Most of the speakers paid little attention to the teenagers setting up taping equipment, checking the microphones, et al. When I stopped by the tape sales table to visit

for a few minutes, I discovered that the tapes and CDs were made by Rhino Technologies, a family business, and the teenagers who had been checking equipment were the children of the company's owner, Mark Reinhardt.

Mark and I talked business for a little bit, and he patiently fielded my questions about various aspects of his business. He explained that they have two teams, and between them they tape more than 100 major events every year. Then he said, "My children have loved hearing your speeches and interacting with you. Would you mind if I give copies to other conference organizers to see if they'll invite you to speak?"

Of course, I told him I didn't mind at all, and I've since received several invitations I believe were the result of Mark's efforts—even though he wasn't "officially" part of the group I had gone to the conference to lead. Turning your charm on and off based on how important you think people are is a sure demonstration that you really *lack* honor, because honor is not an act.

So, cultivate your reputation wherever you are. There are chains of influence and connection everywhere, forming a networking force that determines whether or not you're seen as a credible leader. Your reputation is one of your most prized possessions. In *Richard II*, Shakespeare wrote:

The purest treasure mortal times afford

Is spotless reputation; that away,

Men are but gilded loam or painted clay.

A jewel in a ten-times-barr'd-up chest

Is a bold spirit in a loyal breast.

Mine honour is my life; both grow in one;

Take honour from me, and my life is done.

Accepting Reproof

It was a heartbreaking letter. James (not his real name) had been a leader on his Christian college campus until he was spotted by some classmates breaking one of the most significant rules in the college handbook. James wrote to me in anguish, wondering how he might restore his reputation.

When I wrote back to James, I applauded him for wanting to make things right. Many people, when confronted with their sin, become defiant ("You have no right to judge me!"). But leaders must live by a higher standard altogether—one that points people to truth by the very way they live. To see my specific advice to James, look at the counsel on "Restoring a Damaged Reputation" on page 45.

Carl F. H. Henry, who died in 2003, was one of the great theologians of the twentieth century. He regularly called Christians to the task of Christ-like living with bold statements such as this:

You know a constellation of imperishable values. Live by the mighty truth and power of God. Live above the sludge of a sick society. Live among dispirited humans as the vanguard of peace and good news. Remember, our Commander-in-Chief has no use for tin soldiers.[2]

Proverbs 13:18 points out that "the one who accepts rebuke will be honored." When we've damaged our reputation, we must address it immediately by acknowledging what we've done, finding a way to make it right, and committing to visible change.

Would You Like That Lesson Easy or Hard?

From H. Gene Specht, my high school debate coach, I learned the hard way about accepting reproof. Quite honestly, the man terrified me. Even his name was intimidating. No one knew what the "H" stood for—he wasn't telling, and we didn't ask. Mr. Specht was a feared and admired debate coach, and his reputation had carved out quite a niche for the debate team at Great Bend High School.

We were proud to know our coach was such an amazing guy, but we were also petrified by his booming voice, the way he stared us down during debate rounds, and the manner in which he paused before addressing our questions as if trying to dumb down his replies to fit into our little minds.

Though he could be patronizing, Mr. Specht was the very model of propriety. He took us to the nicest restaurants he could afford on a debate budget and taught us proper manners. He brought in a local clothier to help us learn how to "dress for success." On debate trips, he would drive us past mansions and say, "If you work hard, someday you can succeed and live in homes like these." Pretty materialistic, but it definitely got us thinking about setting high goals.

The greatest lesson I learned from H. Gene Specht, though, was derived from one of the most embarrassing moments of my life. A lesson born out of reproof, I have never forgotten it.

We were returning, in the school van, from a debate trip to Kansas City—the "big city." My partner and I had not fared well. In fact, it was our poorest showing yet, and we were deeply disappointed. As we traveled down Interstate 70, we examined our ballots and mused over our failures. In frustration, I said: "The judges were the worst we've ever had. They just never gave us a chance."

Suddenly, the van swerved to the side of the road. H.Gene Specht, at the wheel, slammed on the brakes, jammed the gearshift into park and removed his seat belt. Turning his laser-like gaze right at me, he boomed: *DON'T YOU E-V-E-R BLAME THE JUDGES FOR YOUR POOR DEBATING!*

Without another word, Mr. Specht turned around, spun the tires and sped back onto the highway.

I wanted to melt through the floor. My classmates sat in embarrassed silence, and I didn't dare meet their gaze. I had been humiliated by the man I admired and feared the most, and it was *not* a nice feeling. In fact, at that moment, I *hated* H. Gene Specht.

But as I thought about it over the next few days, I knew Mr. Specht was right. I had been making excuses rather than taking responsibility. Mr. Specht's reproof had its desired effect on me—and on the other debate team members. We buckled down and were rewarded the following year with victory in the state high school debate championship.

When you mess up, don't make excuses. Make it right.

A Leader's Scars

Even when your reputation is solid, leadership can be costly. Living above reproach may not turn others' hearts toward you. In fact, in our perverse age it may actually turn them against you. You may be lied about. People may even spread malicious rumors about you.

In times like these, your reputation is more important than ever. The Apostle Peter, the brunt of unfair accusations throughout his ministry years, was finally put to death because of his convictions. Before he died, he wrote:

Always be ready to give a defense to anyone who asks you for a reason for the hope that is in you. However, do this with gentleness and respect, keeping your conscience clear, so that when you are accused, those who denounce your Christian life will be put to shame. For it is bet-

"I find it to be most true, that the greatest temptation out of hell is to live without temptations... The devil is but God's master fencer, to teach us to handle our weapons."[3]

—Samuel Rutherford

> "There is a niche which only we can fill, a crown which only we can wear, music which only we can waken, service which only we can render."[4]
>
> —F. B. Meyer

ter to suffer for doing good, if that should be God's will, than for doing evil. (1 Peter 3:15-17)

Peter knew that when his enemies couldn't defeat him fair and square, they would attack him personally. A clear conscience and a gracious spirit wouldn't prevent the attacks, but when they came, God would receive glory and the people making the accusations would be ashamed.

The Price of Greatness Is Responsibility

Winston Churchill said, "The price of greatness is responsibility." Yet very often it is our own followers who launch the most severe attacks. A man from Texas who knew a lot about horses once said to me, "You know, there's a funny thing about stallions in the wild. Their bodies are often deeply scarred."

"Why is that?" I asked. "Are they attacked by wild animals?"

He shook his head. "No, they're viciously kicked by the mares, the very ones they're trying to lead."

Sometimes leadership means being willing to risk everything to make the tough decisions even when people don't understand. And what keeps such ornery followers loyal? The knowledge that you are living above reproof.

Our Lives, Our Fortunes, and Our Sacred Honor

I have the freedom to exercise my leadership gifts because I live in a nation founded by men who sacrificed greatly in order to lead. I've reaped the delicious fruit of their labors all my life even though they had to sacrifice everything during theirs.

Some years ago, I read an Independence Day essay by political activist, Gary Bauer. He called to mind the sacrifice America's early leaders made:

Have you ever wondered what happened to the 56 men who signed the Declaration of Independence? Five signers were captured by the British as traitors and tortured before they died. Twelve had their homes ransacked and burned. Two lost their sons serving in the Revolutionary Army; another had two sons captured. Nine of the 56 fought and died from wounds or hardships of the Revolutionary War. They signed and they pledged their lives, their fortunes, and their sacred honor.

What kind of men were they? Twenty-four were lawyers and jurists. Eleven were merchants, nine were farmers and large plantation owners; men of means, well educated. But they signed the Declaration of Independence knowing full well that the penalty would be death if they were captured.

Carter Braxton of Virginia, a wealthy planter and trader, saw his ships swept from the seas by the British Navy. He sold his home and properties to pay his debts and died in rags. Thomas McKeam was so hounded by the British that he was forced to move his family almost constantly. He served in the Congress without pay and his family was kept in hiding. His possessions were taken from him and poverty was his reward.

Vandals or soldiers looted the properties of Dillery, Hall, Clymer, Walton, Gwinnett, Heyward, Ruttledge, and Middleton. At the battle of Yorktown, Thomas Nelson Jr., noted that the British General Cornwallis had taken over the Nelson home for his headquarters. He quietly urged General George Washington to open fire. The home was destroyed and Nelson died bankrupt.

Francis Lewis had his home and properties destroyed. The enemy jailed his wife, and she died within a few months. John Hart was driven from his wife's bedside as she was dying. Their thirteen children fled for their lives. His fields and his gristmill were laid to waste, he found his wife dead and his children vanished. A few weeks later, he died from exhaustion and a broken heart. Norris and Livingston suffered similar fates. Such were the stories and sacrifices of the American Revolution.

These were not wild-eyed, rabble-rousing ruffians. They were soft-spoken men of means and education. They had security, but they valued liberty more. Standing tall, straight, and unwavering, they pledged: 'For the support of this Declaration, with firm reliance on the protection of the divine providence, we mutually pledge to each other, our lives, our fortunes, and our sacred honor.[5]

I'm glad they made that pledge. Although it cost them dearly, the whole world benefited. That's the essence of leadership: doing the right thing simply because God says so, even though it may never enhance your own personal peace and affluence.

The Value of a Good Reputation

A leader must be above reproach—not perfect but authentically filled with the fruits of a clean conscience. When your followers see that you value your reputation and act in a way that builds respect and demonstrates responsibility, you'll find yourself leading a whole new kind of follower—someone who seeks to follow your example and live in a God-glorifying way.

Notes

1. Pennsylvania Supreme Court. 1815. *The Commonwealth v. Jesse Sharpless and others*, 2 Serg. & R. 91-92, 97, 101-104 (1815).

2. Carl F. H. Henry, *Christian Countermoves in a Decadent Society* (Portland, OR: Multnomah, 1986), p. 144.

3. Samuel Rutherford, *Gleanings from the Past, Vol. I: Extracts from the Letters of Samuel Rutherford*. Selected by Hamilton Smith (London: Central Bible Truth Depot, 1913).

4. F. B. Meyer, *F. B. Meyer: The Best from All His Works*, Charles Erlandson, ed. (Nashville: Thomas Nelson Publishers, 1988), p. 60.

5. Gary Bauer, *End of Day 7/1/2000*. If you would like to receive this update by e-mail or fax, you can sign up online at www.cwfpac.com/cwf_eod_request.htm.

LET'S TALK ABOUT IT

In the video coaching lesson, Dr. Myers said living above reproach means never giving your followers an excuse for living below their God-given potential. List at least 10 ways leaders you've observed have failed to live above reproach.

In the video coaching lesson, Dr. Myers said, "As an emerging leader, when you begin to communicate with other people through encouraging words, you can begin to draw leadership potential out of other people in ways that enhance your credibility and also help them develop their leadership skills." What kind of encouragement do followers need?

(continued on next page)

(continued from previous page)

List the names of five people whom you can encourage this week and two specific things you will say to each person.

COACHING TOOL

Restoring a Damaged Reputation

At some point all leaders make a mistake they heartily wish they could reverse. How can you regain credibility once the damage is done?

1. Identify all the people who have been offended by your actions. Write their names down on a list.

2. Contact each person. Go to each one in person or by telephone (never by e-mail—it's wimpy) and explain what you've done, without offering excuses. Say, "I'm so sorry that my actions affected you. It was thoughtless and insensitive of me, and it has created long-term damage. But can you find it in your heart to forgive me?" Whether they forgive you or not is not as important as having a clean conscience.

3. Seek wise counsel. Find a wise, godly counselor who can hold you accountable for your behavior so you don't make the same mistake twice.

4. Develop a plan for change. In order to trust you again, people will need to see both a spirit of repentance and a dogged determination to do what is right.

5. Don't seek your own interests. Proverbs 27:2 says, "Let another man praise you, and not your own mouth—a stranger, and not your own lips."

Building a Good Reputation

The book of Proverbs contains a wealth of wisdom for leaders. The following references warn against specific things that can destroy your reputation as a leader. Look up each one, and summarize the attack it describes:

1. Proverbs 1:10-19

2. Proverbs 2:22-27

3. Proverbs 3:27-30

4. Proverbs 4:20-27

(continued on next page)

(continued from previous page)

5. Proverbs 5:1-14

6. Proverbs 6:6-11

Being completely honest, what is your reputation with those in your organization right now?
Be specific and descriptive.

Releasing a Behavior that Damages Your Reputation

The following Scripture references describe what you should do when you've sinned. Look up the verses and identify the necessary steps.

1. Psalm 51

2. Matthew 5:21-26

3. Matthew 7:1-5

4. Matthew 18:15-18

VIDEO SESSION: SEEKING THE SOLOMONS

Video Session Four (15 minutes)

Seeking the Solomons

The impact of mentoring on the founding of America

A Simple Mentoring Strategy That Works

• Clarify your _____ or _____

and the _____ you need.

• Search for someone with _____.

• Set out to establish a _____.

• _____ yourself to them: "I've noticed 'X' about your life and would like to take you out for breakfast to ask you some questions."

• Meet in a _____ location. If the meeting goes well, you can repeat it.

• If the relationship seems enjoyable, say: "I would like to be _____ by you in 'X.'"

• Outline specific priorities.

• Suggest a trial period and re-evaluate at the end.

Ensure that you do this for your followers.

CHAPTER FOUR

Seeking the Solomons

KEY QUOTE

**"Mentoring is the 'secret weapon' that really leads
to leadership success."**

CHAPTER AT A GLANCE

Mentoring as a Path to Leadership Success

Video Coaching Session Summary

- The power of mentoring in our history, in business, and in the lives of the next generation of leaders.
- A simple mentoring strategy that really works.

Dynamic Review

- Lost without a map or a clue.
- It may cost you everything—buy it anyway.
- Singing off-key as unto the Lord—how wise mentors help you create a standard of excellence.
- How wise mentors can affirm and help you discover your gifts.
- Feeling accepted and accepting your design.
- Accepting people and motivating them at the same time.
- Mentoring like Jesus.
- A strategy for finding the mentors you need.
- How to begin mentoring others yourself—what to look for and how to grow wise through the experience.
- Five tips for getting the most out of mentoring relationships.

Coaching Tool

- Do you need wise counsel? Follow these six steps to get started.

LOST WITHOUT A MAP OR A CLUE—what an eye-opening experience! I had picked up my rental car at the Newark, New Jersey airport and asked for a map. The representative rudely informed me that a map was already in my car. When I asked *where* in the car it might be, she barked, *"It's above the passenger visor."*

Not wanting to cause further irritation, I found the car, threw my bags into the trunk, and ventured out. Very shortly, I reached above the passenger visor, and, sure enough, I found a map. As I glanced down, however, I was shocked to discover that it was a *Chicago* map, not a *New York City* map.

Don't get me wrong. It was a fine Chicago map. There was nothing wrong with it…except that it was the *wrong* map.

It's easy to recognize when you have the wrong map while driving. But many people are using the wrong map of *life* without knowing it. Maybe they have the wrong map because they got bad advice from an otherwise trustworthy source. Perhaps they had teachers who convinced them of a wrong worldview. Or, as is often the case, they have the wrong map because they trusted themselves rather than asking for directions.

For you to find your way in life you must have accurate directions. And the best directions come from wise counselors who have traveled the route you're on. They know the roadblocks and the pitfalls. We call these people "mentors." In this chapter, we'll examine what mentors can do for you and outline a strategy for getting the mentoring you need.

Whatever Else You Get, Be Sure to Get What Matters Most

There are three important facts your map of life must tell you:

Where you are,

Where you are going, and

How to get there.

If any of these pieces of information is missing, you'll never arrive at your life purpose. What you need is a guidance system, a system the Bible calls *wisdom*. Proverbs 4:7 says, "Wisdom is supreme— so get wisdom. And whatever else you get, get understanding."

Wisdom isn't something you pick up on your own, and it can't be learned from a cartoonish guru meditating at the top of some mountain. You need real world, practical wisdom—the kind formed in the crucible of everyday experience. The only way to get that wisdom is by listening to wise counsel.

Flip open a Bible to the book of Proverbs and start reading randomly. You'll very quickly be struck with the realization that wisdom is only gained by paying attention and listening to wise people. Here's what I mean:

- 1:8—Listen, my son, to your father's instruction.

- 3:1—My son, don't forget my teaching.

- 4:1—Listen, my sons, to a father's discipline.

- 4:10—Listen, my son. Accept my words.

- 4:20—My son, pay attention to my words.

- 5:1—My son, pay attention to my wisdom, listen closely to my understanding.

- 7:1—My son, obey my words, and treasure my commands.

- 7:24—Now, my sons, listen to me, and pay attention to the words of my mouth.

- 22:17—Listen closely, pat attention to the words of the wise.

- 23:19—Listen, my son, and be wise.

- 23:26—My son, give me your heart, and let your eyes observe my ways.

"Mentor," the popular term for wise counselor, is the name Homer gave Odysseus' spiritual guide and caretaker of Odysseus' son in *The Odyssey.* It means "a close companion or guide who helps a person make wise decisions about life."

Paul Stanley and Bobby Clinton define mentoring as, "a relational experience in which one person empowers another by sharing God-given goals."[1] In their study of mentoring, Stanley and Clinton examined 600 leaders in a variety of fields over eight years. Almost all of these leaders identified three to ten people who contributed significantly to their growth as leaders. These influencers seemed to share six characteristics:

- Ability to see potential in a person;

- Tolerance with mistakes, brashness, abrasiveness, and the like in order to see that potential develop;

- Flexibility in responding to people and circumstances;

- Patience, knowing that time and experience are needed for development;

- Perspective, having vision and ability to see down the road and suggest the next steps that a mentoree needs;

- Gifts and abilities that build up and encourage others.[2]

Mentoring is vital to your success. A person cannot be a leader without mentoring others, and one cannot become a leader without having others mentor him or her. To paraphrase Howard Hendricks, distinguished professor at Dallas Theological Seminary, every leader needs a Paul (a person to be their mentor), a Timothy (a person they can influence), and a Barnabas (a peer who can encourage and build them up).

Why? Because wise mentors can provide a map with all three key points: where you are, where you need to be, and how to get to your destination. Let's look at each one of these in turn.

Mentors Show You Where You Are

Mentors can help you discover your God-given gifts and design. You can't lead effectively without some basic insight into *how* and *why* you lead. In other words, you must know *where you are* before you set out for a destination.

Five Tips for Getting the Most Out of Mentoring Relationships

(1) Always maintain a learning posture.

Keep a notebook and pen with you at all times. In speeches or meetings, take notes. If someone recommends a book with valuable info, get it and read it. If someone suggests calling a person, do so.

(2) Seek several mentors.

There are very few "grand-daddy" mentors who can answer all your questions. Try to find different mentors for different aspects of your life.

(3) Always take the initiative.

Suggest specific times you could meet. Demonstrate leadership by paying for meals or beverages when together.

(4) Don't use the word "mentoring"!

Paul Stanley, co-author of the book *Connecting*, notes that the word "mentoring" scares people. They feel overwhelmed and under-qualified. Ask for feedback, coaching, suggestions...just not mentoring!

(5) Build in a natural sunset to the relationship.

If someone asked me to be their "mentor for life" (one popular book actually suggests this) I would be scared away. But if someone says, "I'd like to meet with you three times in the next six weeks to talk about 'X'," I'd be a lot more likely to say "yes." If the relationship continues, great, but if not, neither of you will feel tied down.

Last summer when I shared the story about my Chicago map in New York City, an older gentleman in the audience made an enlightening observation that expanded on my analogy. Visiting a foreign city, he had been presented with a fine map of his surroundings, his intended destination clearly marked. "There was only one thing missing," he said. "I had no idea where I *was*. Without that crucial piece of information, my meticulously drawn map was worthless."

Excellent point. When I told my map story I was thinking about being lost because I didn't know how to get where I was *going*. But the fact is you must also know your starting point. If you don't know where you *are*, you can't know how to set a course for where you want to go.

The postmodern worldview teaches that *you* are in charge. Whatever *you* feel is real, *is* real. Whatever *you* want to be true, *is* true. *You* can be whatever you want to be, and as the cloying children's program *Blues Clues* informs its impressionable viewers, "You can do anything that *you* want to do."

I'm sure the purveyors of this philosophy mean well. After all, don't we want to encourage excellence by helping people feel good about themselves?

Not exactly. Excellence does not come from being the best you *think* you can be or by rising to a level where those around you think you are terrific. Excellence comes from: (1) being accepted for who God designed you to be and

(2) being challenged to boost your performance to match your potential.

Imagine how silly it would be to think your paintings should be hung in an art gallery because your first-grade teacher said you were the best artist in her class. Or contemplate for a moment the reaction you would get if you went to the Olympic marathon trials saying, "When I was nine, I beat every girl in my class in a running race. Therefore, I am the best." What you need instead are significant others who recognize and appreciate your design and know how to lead you to excellence.

By pulling us away from our foundation in God, or any higher values at all, the postmodern mindset has committed identity theft on a grand scale. Unsure of where we are, we have no sense of where to go or how to get there.

This is where a good mentor comes in big time. He or she will communicate acceptance in a way that drives you toward positive change. To realize your full potential, you need someone who can help you learn, grow, stretch, sweat, strive, and wear yourself out pursuing an objective standard that lies outside of yourself.

Mentors Show Where You Need to Be

I hate asking for directions. My wife would say that it's because I'm a guy, and guys *always* hate asking for directions. But maybe it's also because I've gotten so many *bad* directions. I've tried to pry directions from people who didn't speak English, people who were

> "...my desire is not to convince you to finish everything. My desire is to encourage you to finish the right thing."[3]
>
> —Max Lucado

"Concerning all acts of initiative (and creation), there is one elementary truth the ignorance of which kills countless ideas and splendid plans: that the moment one definitely commits oneself, then Providence moves too."[9]

—W.H. Murray

just guessing, people who didn't know where they were *themselves*, and people whose bravado masked the fact that they didn't know—"Just hang a right, then a left, then two rights, then three lefts, then three more lefts. *CAN'T MISS IT.*" The next thing I know, I've missed my destination by half a state and am well on my way to Dodge City!

To get good directions, you have to ask someone who knows. And who is most likely to know? *Someone who regularly goes where you're going and knows what it takes to get there.* If you're accustomed to asking for directions from well-meaning people who *like* you but don't have any idea how to get you to your destination, you'll never arrive.

Singing Off-Key as Unto the Lord

The principle of not knowing where you are can be illustrated by an experience I once had as the guest speaker in a church. The service featured an energetic young soloist I'll call Tiffany. She belted out a love song to Jesus as best she could while reading the lyrics off the accompanying J-card. If Tiffany had any potential—and I certainly don't mean to be insensitive—her potential stayed home that morning. Imagine my surprise when Tiffany received a sustained round of applause, complete with men booming "Amen!" and women shouting out, "Sing it, sister!" She beamed and bowed graciously before descending from the podium.

Given her lack of vocal talent, I was astounded at how smitten the folks

in the church were with Tiffany. One parishioner, a gregarious man of retirement age enthused, "That girl is our best singer—she's so good!" Most of the others in the congregation seemed to understand that Tiffany's gifts were not in music, but they were too embarrassed or ill-equipped to help her discover her genuine gifts.

Later as I reflected on Tiffany's situation, I realized that perhaps the folks in the church thought this girl was a great singer because they thought she was a great *person*. Tiffany clearly was gifted in her relationships with people, and God had given her favor with many in the congregation. But they would have benefited Tiffany more by accepting her unconditionally and then helping her discover her true God-given gifts.

Whether or not someone is a great singer is not something that can be properly judged without musical training. Please understand: if I stood up there and sang, people would roll their eyes, to say the least. Pavarotti I'm not. But even *I* can tell you that if Tiffany, buoyed by the enthusiasm of the congregation, tries to cut a CD or major in music at college, she'll be in for a shock.

At some point in our lives, we must enlist people to affirm us and inventory our gifts so we get a stronger sense of what God wants us to do.

Feeling Accepted and Accepting Your Design

It's discouraging to think we can't be anything we want to be. It may even seem cruel to tell someone that. But how much more cruel is it to be led on by visions of grandeur, only to discover that we don't stack up?

Of course, truth-telling doesn't have to be obnoxious, like the man who brought himself to say, "Thank you" to a soloist who had just shared one of her own passionate but mediocre songs. The soloist replied rapturously, "I soooo appreciate your saying so because the Lord gave that song to me."

To which the man replied, "Oh, I wouldn't be so sure. I imagine He can write a lot better songs than *that*!"

Finding your true gifts enables you to thrive. Consider the contrast between Tiffany and a lady I met while preparing for the keynote address at a conference of the Christian Home Educators of Colorado. I had noticed upon arriving that the staging, sound, and video were being handled in a professional, gracious manner by a company called Sound on Sound. I sought out the owners, David and Debra Hash, and, in talking with them, I asked Debra how she got into the business.

Debra said with infectious glee, "Well, I always wanted to be on stage, up in front of people. But I couldn't sing, and I couldn't act. I had a chance to try event production, and I loved it. So our family started this business. Now I get to be part of the excitement of an event and showcase the talents of others. God gave me the desires of my heart once I focused on living out my design."

Debra understood her design and enjoyed living it out. God had truly given her the desires of her heart.

What Is True Acceptance?

Have you ever met people who have built up false expectations because they don't have anyone in their lives to recognize and affirm their true gifts? Such people court failure because of misunderstanding why they're on this planet in the first place. In the meantime, the things God *did* design them to do never get done because they invest their lives trying to live out someone else's gifts.

One of the reasons people develop visions of grandeur is that they haven't been affirmed in what they actually *can* do. Wise mentors can help you avoid this tragedy. They can affirm your value while painting a picture of what true excellence looks like for you. They can help draw out your gifts while gently pushing you out of your nest so you can learn to fly. They can help you see the difference between your strengths and weaknesses, gifts and vain ambitions, insights and blind spots.

Accepting people means acknowledging that they are divinely created, unique persons with inestimable value. It also means recognizing that they are only living out a fraction of their gifts and living up to only a small part of their potential. Both of these things are necessary for inspirational living.

> "Concerning all acts of initiative (and creation), there is one elementary truth the ignorance of which kills countless ideas and splendid plans: that the moment one definitely commits oneself, then Providence moves too."[9]
>
> —W.H. Murray

Accepting People and Motivating Them at the Same Time

I need to mention a crucial point here that touches on the subject of accepting and motivating people. Some leaders fear that accepting people just the way they are will take away their motivation to excel. Actually, the opposite is true, as Bill Thrall and his co-authors emphasize in *The Ascent of a Leader*:

> If people affirm us for who we are, this ignites a desire to please them. If we love and are loved in spite of what we know about others or what they know about us, we become empowered to change for the better…. Practicing acceptance does not mean we abandon performance standards or accountability in our organizations…. An organization without accountability is a ship without a rudder. But to maintain a basis for healthy accountability, the organization must also accept its role as a community.[4]

By accepting and challenging their team members, everyday leaders have the power to motivate them to great deeds.

Mentors Help You Find Your Destination

"This could be the best year of your life or the worst year of your life, depending on whether you listen to me."

That's the first thing I ever remember Dr. Mary Rowland saying to me. As you might expect, I found her maternal bossiness unnerving. Dr. Rowland was Vice President for Student Life, the one charged with making sure student government officials did not abuse their power.

But I was the newly elected student government president, ready to show my independence from the university's administration. My friends even encouraged me, "Don't listen to Dr. Rowland—she's just trying to control you."

The fact is, however, I didn't have a clue about what I was doing. With a one-vote margin of victory, my hold on power was tenuous, and warring factions of student groups were eager to do battle. I knew where I wanted to go and had a budget of several hundred thousand dollars to work with, but I had no idea how to get there.

So, I listened to Dr. Rowland. A strong mentor, Dr. Rowland helped me establish a strategic plan and make peace between various campus groups. She introduced me to college officials and government leaders. She even coaxed the maintenance crew into upgrading our shabby student government offices.

As a result, our student government experienced unprecedented unity. We accomplished valuable projects that, to this day, still benefit students at Washburn University.

Dr. Rowland taught me first-hand the benefits of mentoring. I *experienced* what can happen when a leader invests in the life of an emerging leader. I *bene-fited* from the encouragement and guid-ance of Dr. Rowland's friendship.

All told, Dr. Rowland invested about thirty hours in my life during that year, time that dramatically advanced my own leadership ability, transformed our student government, and equipped me to coach two successive student govern-ment administrations.

The success of our student govern-ment contributed to Dr. Rowland's suc-cess, too. She received credit from the administration when things went well. She also found more freedom to pursue her other goals.

But for Dr. Rowland, mentoring went beyond coaching and counseling to become sponsorship and friendship. She helped me get into graduate school. Her notes of encouragement and phone calls kept me motivated.

About a year after my graduation, however, I received the shocking news that Dr. Rowland had died from a brain aneurysm at the age of 48. Dr. Rowland didn't influence me because of the cur-riculum she taught or the position she held. She *lived* leadership in front of me. She coached me until I became the leader I was meant to be. That's what wise mentors do. They help you catch a vision of where you need to be, and they show you how to get there.

Mentoring Like Jesus

When Dr. Rowland died, I asked to write the tribute in our alumni maga-zine. In my article I said, in essence, "Mary Rowland led as Jesus led." I

didn't have any vague, mushy sentiment in mind when I said that—I meant it quite literally. Gunter Krallmann in his book *Mentoring for Missions*, calls Jesus' leadership style "with-ness" and says:

Through the disciples' continual exposure to who he was, what he did and said, Jesus intended them to discern and absorb his vision, mindset and mode of operation. He desired them to become so saturated with the influences arising from his example and teaching, his attitudes, actions, and anointing, that every single area of their lives would be impacted toward greater likeness to himself.[5]

The greatest lessons in life are *caught* not *taught*. Jesus didn't just teach, He took people with him everywhere he went and let his life soak into theirs un-til it literally changed their character—they began to act and talk like Him.

I can testify personally that relational experiences are an effective way to equip others. In college, I interned for an advertising agency. I was assigned to the department that buys advertising time on television and radio stations. My supervisor didn't have the foggiest idea of how to mentor, but her instincts were right. She said, "Just put your desk outside my office door and listen to everything that happens." While doing my own work, I overheard her conver-sations and learned effective negotiation skills.

Jesus lived a life that inspired his followers to carry his message all over

> **75% of Fortune 500 executives said that mentoring was a major key to their success.**

the world. As an everyday leader and a child of the King, you can learn from that example.

Are You Mentoring Others?

Mentors really do make a difference. Studies of mentoring aimed at troubled youth have concluded that having an older, wiser guide dramatically decreases the drop-out rate, dramatically increases the number of students seeking further education, increases students' GPA, and boosts students' reading scores.

These mentors were not professionals— they were ordinary people like you and me, ranging from high school peers to retired persons.[6]

It's no wonder that 75% of Fortune 500 executives said mentoring was a major key to their success and that the vast majority of profitable companies identified mentoring as their preferred way to make learning happen in their organizations.[7]

In addition to seeking people to be your mentors, have you thought about "paying it forward" by mentoring others? Consider the impact you could have, even if you are only a few steps ahead of someone else.

The Most Influential of His Generation

One of the most heart-warming stories about how ordinary people can have an extraordinary influence is told by Robert Greenleaf, the author of *Servant Leadership*. He studied the effec-

tiveness of twelve AT&T executives, all of whom said they had been intentionally mentored and guided into positions of influence.

Remarkably, four of these executives had been mentored by the same man. Upon further examination, Greenleaf discovered that this one man, a mid-level manager (one of 900 people at his level), *had been responsible for training literally one-third of the top management of AT&T.*[8]

If you know anything about how big AT&T is, you'll understand just how stunning this statistic is. Greenleaf called this manager "the most influential manager of his generation" because of his phenomenal mentoring influence.

That could be *you*, by God's grace. Is it possible that God wants you to strive for being the most influential teacher in your school? The most influential student at your college? The most influential youth leader in your church? It doesn't come from being the one who makes all the decisions and gets it all done. It comes from building into the lives of those who someday *will* make all the decisions and get it all done.

Whom Should You Invest In?

Nowhere is the need for mentoring greater than in the church, where mentoring is usually called discipleship and deemed important only for helping people develop a closer walk with God. Discipleship, however, used to have a more full-bodied meaning: to teach people to obey God in every area in which Jesus Christ has authority (this is everywhere, by the way).

How do you decide who to invest your time in? Tim Elmore, vice-president of EQUIP, offers a helpful tool by using the acrostic "FAITH":

F = Faithful. Is this person faithful to commitments, as well as to the basics of the Christian faith?

A = Available. Does this person have the time and availability to make growth opportunities a priority?

I = Initiative. Does this person show initiative in the desire to grow—to take the first step without someone "holding their hand"?

T = Teachable. Is this person willing to learn new truths, be open to change, and exhibit a "soft" heart? Will he or she learn from you?

H = Hungry. Does this person have a passion to grow and a hunger for intimacy with God?[10]

Millions of people are bursting with Kingdom-building potential, and mentoring in all its forms—discipleship, coaching, teaching, and modeling—is the way to unleash that potential. It's such a significant point that Dietrich Bonhoeffer, the German pastor martyred by Adolph Hitler, wrote, "Christianity without discipleship is Christianity without Christ."[11]

How Will You Know if You're Growing Wise?

I often hear people say, "My actions are not right, but my intentions are good—I'm really a good person at heart." In other words, it's not what I *do* but how I see myself that counts. The biblical idea of wisdom flatly contradicts this kind of thinking. The Hebrew word for wisdom is "khokmah," which roughly translates "skill." As Proverbs 20:11 says, "Even a young man is known by his actions—by whether his behavior is pure and upright."

Your actions arise from your heart. If you act wisely, it's an indication your heart is becoming wise. If your actions are foolish, you have a foolish heart and desperately need to buy wisdom.

The focus on right action is especially important when finding mentors or when mentoring others. Your goal is not to be perfect, but to align your motives and actions so that wisdom grows in the soil of your life. Lawrence O. Richards explains:

> A wise person is one who is sensitive to the Lord and who subjects himself to God. A wise person will apply guidelines revealed by God and make his daily decisions based on these truths. In its deepest meaning 'wisdom' unites God's words and everyday experience, and it is only in the way a person lives his life that wisdom can be demonstrated.[12]

Be honest with yourself and those who look to you for guidance. Affirm that "my goal for myself is to move

Proverbs 31: 23, 31 – "Her husband is known at the city gates, where he sits among the elders of the land…. let her works praise her at the city gates."

Proverbs 24:7 – "Wisdom is inaccessible to a fool; he does not open his mouth at the gate."

Proverbs 13:20 – "The one who walks with the wise will become wise, but a companion of fools will suffer harm."

from foolishness to wisdom, and that's my goal for you, too."

The Old Testament test for wisdom was whether your words would be seen as wise "in the city gate." In those days, kings and rulers made their judgments publicly, in front of the citizens and foreign visitors. Whether the decisions were wise or foolish would immediately be evident to all. Therefore, a wise man or woman would be respected and praised at the city gates (Proverbs 31:23, 31), and a fool would be silent at the city gate in order to avoid displaying his ignorance (Proverbs 24:7).

Leaders face the greatest scrutiny of all. It's a good thing—it sharpens you and equips you for effective action. But it makes it all the more important to seek the Solomons in your life, so that by walking with the wise you may grow wise (Proverbs 13:20).

A Strategy for Finding the Mentors You Need

The video coaching session, "Seeking the Solomons," gives you a strategy for finding those who can mentor you effectively. My leadership students have found this process to be extremely helpful in identifying mentors, so it's worth reviewing here in greater detail.

(1) *Clarify your challenge or task and the skills you need.* To be successful you'll need mentoring in your vocation, your spiritual life, and your life skills (relationships, parenting, etc.). Make a list of those you admire who have made wise decisions in these areas.

Your list should be as detailed as possible.

(2) *Search for someone with experience.* Don't look for the "perfect" person. Just find someone who knows more than you do. If you are new to a job, for example, ask others, "Who is respected and really knows the job well?"

(3) *Set out to establish a relationship.* There are many ways you can introduce yourself to a potential mentor:

• [After introducing yourself] "I've noticed 'X' about your life and am very impressed with the way you have succeeded with integrity. I would like to take you out to breakfast Tuesday morning at 7:00 for an hour to ask you ten questions about what you do. Will that work in your schedule?"

• [To a supervisor] "I've been here in this job for a while, and I know that you once held my position. Could I take you to lunch this Wednesday at noon to get some specific feedback on ways I can improve?"

• [To a successful co-worker or classmate] "I've noticed that you're really accomplished at 'X.' Could I buy lunch today and get some pointers from you on how you do it?"

(4) *Arrange a meeting.* Restaurants usually work best because they are non-threatening and people have to eat anyway. Plus, successful leaders are accustomed to discussing important topics over meals. I prefer breakfast because it's the cheapest meal of the day at any restaurant, and it doesn't interfere with the rest of my daily plans. Here are some quick tips about common courtesy at such meetings:

• Give your mentor's convenience preference over your own. If the only time the person can meet is 5:30 a.m., then you'll need to get up early enough to be alert and on time. Too difficult? Then you probably don't want it badly enough.

• It is absolutely essential that *you* pay for the other person's meal. They're giving valuable time, and you'll show maturity and appreciation by picking up the tab. You may have to speak to your server in advance, but make sure that when the check comes, it comes to you.

(5) *Ask for coaching.* Make a list of thoughtful questions you can ask the other person. Here are some suggestions:

• "What made the difference for you?"

• "I'd like to hear the story about how you got into _____."

• "What are the most important lessons you've learned along the way?"

• "If you had it to do over again, what would you do differently?"

• "What advice would you give to someone getting into this field today?"

• "Who are the key leaders in this field that I should be paying attention to?"

• "Who are some of the people who personally influenced you toward success?"

• "What are the five books you have found most helpful in this field?"

• "Are there any magazines or publications I need to be reading on a regular basis?"

• "What are the essential principles for success in this field?"

• "Time and money aside, what would you rather be doing?"

• "What are your goals at the present time?"

• "Do you have a yearly planning process? If so, how does it work?"

• "How do you manage your time successfully?"

• "Have you ever coached anyone else to be successful in this field?"

• "What are some ways I can learn more about this field?"

• "What are some of the obstacles along the way that I'll need to be aware of?"

• "What made the difference for you as you sought to be successful?"

(and my all-time favorite last question)

• "What questions have I not asked that I should be asking?"

(6) *Suggest further meetings.* If the relationship seems enjoyable for both of you, say, "I would like to be coached by you in 'X.'" Be as specific as you can. For instance, "I've learned so much this morning—I've got two whole pages of notes! But our conversation has actually brought up several other questions about _____. I'd like to get a little coaching from you on it. Would you mind getting together again for an hour, same time, same place—next week?"

(7) *Outline priorities.* If the relationship progresses, outline things you would like to learn and establish specific priorities.

(8) *Suggest a trial period.* Always include a time-frame so the other person doesn't feel weighed down by the relationship. For example, "I'd like to get some coaching from you on how to become a producer in the recording industry. Could we meet once a week for six weeks at this same time, for you to coach me? At the end of that time I'd like to have my application to the training program complete so you can evaluate it. I'd also like to have a one-year plan for how to move toward success. Will that work for you?"

This eight-step process will serve you well. Of course, you may need to make adjustments to it here and there, but as I said in the video, the money I've spent to buy breakfast for others is the best investment I've ever made.

One final note here: in order to be above reproach, it is best for men to mentor men and women to mentor women. In the workplace it will be different, of course. But when it comes to life-on-life issues, same-sex mentoring is the best policy. If you're a woman and need counsel from a man, invite him to join a group of both men and women to share his expertise. Be persistent, but be wise.

Notes

1. Paul D. Stanley and J. Robert Clinton, *Connecting: The Mentoring Relationships You Need to Succeed in Life* (Colorado Springs, CO: NavPress, 1992), p. 38.

2. Ibid.

3. Max Lucado, *Just Like Jesus* (Nashville: Word, 1998), pp. 154-155.

4. Bill Thrall, Bruce McNicol, and Ken McElrath, *The Ascent of a Leader* (San Francisco: Jossey-Bass, 1999), pp. 52-53.

5. Gunter Krallmann, *Mentoring for Mission* (Waynesboro, GA: Gabriel, 2002), p. 53.

6. Robert D. Putnam and Lewis M. Feldstein, *Better Together: Restoring the American Community* (New York: Simon and Schuster, 2003), p. 201.

7. Australian Mentoring Institute's Peer Mentoring Program documents cite this statistic,

apparently referenced in a study done by the American Society for Training and Development.

8. Robert Greenleaf, *Servant Leadership: A Journey into the Nature of Legitimate Power and Greatness* (Mahwah, NJ: Paulist Press, 2002).

9. W. H. Murray, *The Scottish Himalaya Expedition*, 1951.

10. Tim Elmore, *Mentoring: How to Invest Your Life in Others* (Duluth, GA: Equip, 1998), p. 60.

11. Dietrich Bonhoeffer, *Cost of Discipleship* (New York: Touchstone, 1995), p. 46.

12. Lawrence O. Richards, *The Teacher's Commentary* (Wheaton, IL: Victor Books, 1987).

LET'S TALK ABOUT IT

Who are three positive influencers in your life? What have you learned from each of them? What lessons from their lives could you pass on to others?

Have you had any negative influencers in your life? What have you learned from each of them? What lessons from their lives could you warn other people against?

(continued on next page)

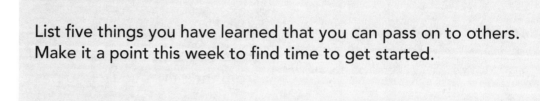

(continued from previous page)

List five things you have learned that you can pass on to others. Make it a point this week to find time to get started.

Dr. Myers perceives that many people are trying to become good at things they aren't gifted to do while ignoring or misunderstanding their God-given gifts. Do you see this happening? If so, why do you think it happens?

Thinking about the life of Christ, what are some of the things He did to mentor His disciples? How could you accomplish these same things in the life of another person?

COACHING TOOL

Six steps to get the mentoring you need

Getting someone to mentor you isn't hard. It just takes a little planning and persistence. Follow these six steps to get started.

Step 1: Check your gut.

How badly do you want mentoring? Check "yes" or "no" on the following questions:

Am I committed to growing?   Yes   No
Am I open to receiving instruction?   Yes   No
Am I willing to use mistakes as a platform for growth?   Yes   No

If you answered "no" to any of these questions, you're not ready for mentoring. Pray that God will open your heart and make you teachable.

Step 2: Identify the barriers that stand in the way.

What difficulties do you regularly face that prevent you from living wholeheartedly? Check each one that applies, and then on the line next to that item put the name of a person who seems to have broken through that barrier. For example, if you checked "I'm under stress," write down someone you know who manages stress well. Keep thinking and praying until you have at least one name, preferably two, next to each checked item.

_____ I've run into problems I can't solve.   _____

_____ I can't seem to get organized.   _____

_____ I don't understand what to do.   _____

_____ I've run out of ideas.   _____

_____ I need more information.   _____

_____ I'm experiencing conflict.   _____

_____ I don't know what I need to know.   _____

_____ I lack direction.   _____

_____ I'm fearful.   _____

_____ I'm discouraged.   _____

_____ I'm trapped by memories of past failures.   _____

_____ I don't manage my time well.   _____

_____ I lack self-discipline   .   _____

_____ I'm hurting from past wounds.   _____

_____ I'm overloaded   .   _____

_____ I'm under stress.   _____

_____ I'm exhausted.   _____

(continued on next page)

(continued from previous page)

Step 3: Devise your game plan.

Check the questions you'd like to ask those whose names you wrote above:

_____ "You succeeded where most have failed. What made the difference for you?"

_____ "I'd like to hear your story about how you overcame [barrier] ."

_____ "If you had it to do over again, what would you do differently?"

_____ "Who are some of the people who personally influenced you toward success?"

_____ "Who do you know who can help me with [barrier] ?"

_____ "What books you have found most helpful in overcoming [barrier] ?"

_____ "What would you say are the essential principles for success in this field?"

_____ "What steps should I take to overcome [barrier] ?"

_____ "Have you ever coached anyone else to be successful in overcoming [barrier] ?"

_____ "What obstacles will prevent me from successfully overcoming [barrier] ?"

Step 4: Follow through.

Get in contact with your potential mentor. Here are the most common strategies and their likelihood of success.

***** (5 stars) Personal contact. Talk to the person face to face and express your interest in learning from him or her. Ask for a meeting so you can ask your questions.

**** (4 stars) Letter. Write a letter to the person and mail or fax it. Most people receive little personal mail, so this usually works well. Follow up with a phone call.

*** (3 stars) Telephone call. Phone calls are semi-personal, but busy people don't take calls from folks they don't know. For best results, establish personal contact first.

** (2 stars) E-mail. Use e-mail only if your question can be answered in a simple sentence or two. For best results, follow up if you have not heard back in a week.

* (1 star) One-time contact. Contacting a person just one time, no matter your method, is a recipe for failure. Demonstrate that you are serious by being politely persistent.

(continued on next page)

(continued from previous page)

Step 5: Follow up.

Express appreciation by giving your mentor specific feedback. For example, "Thank you for taking time to meet with me to talk about 'X.' I learned 'Y' and 'Z' from our time together and have begun to put your advice into practice in the following ways..."

Step 6: Keep these key points in mind.

- Mentoring is more like dating than marriage. Focus your expectations on learning rather than gaining a long-term commitment from your mentor.

- Know when to give up. If you can't connect after three tries, it means that the person is not interested or available. Go to the next person on your list.

- Make it convenient. Find ways to spend time with your mentor that are not disruptive to his or her schedule. And remember: If you meet over a meal, pick up the check!

- Repeat often. Being mentored is not a one-time thing. Wise people repeat the process regularly with lots of different mentors.

- Act! Nothing frustrates a potential mentor more than giving advice to someone who never learns. Act on what you learn and let him or her know!

- Whatever you do, don't call the person a mentor. The term "mentoring" scares people. It's best just to get the wise counsel you need and leave it at that.

VIDEO SESSION: HOW TO BE A GOOD FOLLOWER

Video Session Five (14 minutes)

Four Steps to Being a Good Follower

(1) Be _____.

(2) Understand the leader.

    • What does he or she _____?

    • What _____ him or her?

    • Where does he or she _____ _____ _____?

(3) Be _____.

(4) Maintain the _____.

CHAPTER FIVE

How to Be a Good Follower

KEY QUOTE
**"How good a leader you are depends in large measure
on how well you follow."**

CHAPTER AT A GLANCE

The Essence of True Leadership

Video Coaching Session Summary
- 4 steps to being a good follower.
- How to employ godly persuasion to lead when you're not in charge.

Dynamic Review
- It's not about leadership—it's about followership.
- You gotta serve somebody.
- 4 proven methods for developing leadership through "followership."
- How to be a trustworthy follower.
- Making the boss successful.
- Avoiding the disasters that plague most followers.
- How to persuade your leader to do what is right.
- What to do when your leader is preventing your success.
- Fleeing the integrity killers.
- Don't do as the Vulcans do.
- You may have to be a bit creative.
- How to make a persuasive appeal.
- Are you being defensive?

Coaching Tool
- Are you in the in-group or the out-group? Use this tool to measure your followership.

IT'S NOT JUST ABOUT LEADERSHIP. It's also about *followership.*

Some time ago I met Jessica (not her real name), a Christian taking a speech class at her local community college. When asked to give a persuasive speech, she chose to convince audience members that they are sinners.

As you can imagine, the professor was deeply offended ("So you think you're the judge of what's right and wrong?") and graded her speech accordingly. Moreover, her classmates banded together in an angry rebuttal. Unfortunately, the speech was the first in a series of three on that same subject.

"I'm doomed," Jessica thought, dreading her next encounter with the class.

After praying about it, Jessica had a change of heart. She recognized that, in the context of the class, the professor was her leader—with legitimate authority—and, as a student, Jessica owed respect to the professor. Jessica realized that if she changed her tactics and was more responsive to the professor's authority, she would have a golden opportunity to demonstrate the grace that is the solution to the problem of sin.

For Jessica, working through this process wasn't so much about how she *led* as about how she *followed*. Here's a truth about leadership that applies to every situation in life: how good a leader you are depends in large measure upon how well you follow.

After the professor's disappointing response to her speech, Jessica asked me how she might redeem herself. In this chapter, I'll share the counsel I gave Jessica because I believe it will help you become more successful as a leader in the difficult circumstances of your life—whether in school, at work, in relationships, or as a citizen.

You Gotta Serve Somebody

Everyone is under the authority of someone—bosses, teachers, parents, police officers, judges, or elected of-ficials. No matter where you are in life, you have to follow somebody whether you like them or not. As the folk singer, Bob Dylan, poignantly noted, "You gotta serve somebody."

Many Christians believe that, because Christianity opposes seculariation, we are justified in rebelling against authority. Liberation theologians even claim that Jesus' withering criticism of religious leaders and compassion for the downtrodden made him a proto-Marxist revolutionary. Following Jesus' model of leadership presumably means to these theologians that we should take charge by overthrowing our authorities.

I've even met people who are under the impression that laws favoring abortion and other moral atrocities invalidate the government's authority. In their minds, this makes it okay to commit all manner of unlawful acts, from cheating on taxes, to infringing copyrights, to disobeying traffic laws.

We have a leadership crisis today because we have a crisis of authority. Each person feels he is a law unto himself, owing allegiance to no one else. Such people cannot follow ("Who are *you* to tell *me* what to do?"), nor can they lead ("Who am *I* to tell *you* what to do?"). They may whine a lot, but they'll never change anything for the better.

Once you make up your mind to be a good follower, however, a whole world of leadership influence opens up.

Four Proven Methods for Developing Leadership Through "Followership"

To lead with integrity means you lead in full understanding of your place as a follower. Those who wield authority with wisdom know how to do so because they, too, are under authority. Those who use their power justly do so because they know that power is borrowed currency, every penny of which must be accounted for someday. Even powerful CEOs report to boards of directors, and the "most powerful man on the planet," the President of the United States, holds office only by the will of the American people.

We have a name for those who attempt to become leaders without being good followers: dictators. Such people use their power to manipulate and intimidate, crushing all opposition. But when the resources and power fade, followers swallow their fear and angrily strip the dictators of power. It's happened thousands of times throughout history in governments, business, and churches.

Do you want to be an effective leader? Then earn the love of those you lead. Ultimately, the power of love is the only power worth having. Lead from a position of "followership" if you desire long-term impact.

Through my years of leadership, I've seen God's principles demonstrated time and again. Specifically, I've no-ticed there are four followership qualities that successful leaders carry with them on their way to the top:

(1) Be trustworthy;

(2) Make sure the leader is more successful because of your followership;

(3) Find creative ways to make your organization successful; and

(4) Nurture and strengthen your relationship with your leader.

If you're ready to become an excellent follower, then I predict you'll quickly become the kind of leader God wants you to be.

Followership Principle #1: Be Trustworthy

"No matter what," I told Jessica after hearing the story of her speech class disaster, "keep your cool when you give your next speech. Be pleasant, have an eager attitude, and work hard, and you'll win the respect of all but the most hostile professor." I suggested that she demonstrate trustworthiness by completing her course work with excellence and striving to learn as much as possible. What better testimony can a Christian have than to be absolutely, completely trustworthy in all she does?

One of my favorite books is entitled, *Getting It Done: How to Lead When You're Not in Charge* by Roger Fisher and Alan Sharp. The very title of the book presents a paradox: you're never really in charge, but you're called to exercise leadership anyway. And you can't succeed unless you pull it off.

Trust doesn't come from talk. Those who constantly say "Trust me" probably can't be trusted. They're like Kaa, the boa constrictor in Disney's *Jungle Book: The Movie.* He sings "Trust in Me" to lull Mowgli to sleep so he can eat the boy.

Trustworthiness usually comes down to three questions you need to answer with a "yes": Will you demonstrate responsibility in doing the right thing? Will you respond with integrity when you don't agree with decisions the leader has made? Will you enhance the leader's ability to move in a God-honoring direction?

Let's take a look at each of these in turn.

(1) Do the Right Thing. The secret to good followership is to cultivate a lifestyle of credibility. In Chapter 3, we discussed how to become credible with your followers, but you also need to become credible with those in authority over you. Don't wait to start refining your credibility until you're in trouble. Instead, develop that reputation *now.* Leaders who do so quickly become indispensable.

Doing the right thing means sticking to your task until it's completed. Don't make excuses or harbor bitterness. In-stead, become a problem-solver and trusted advisor. Ultimately you won't need to say much—leaders will see that you're reliable and wise, and they'll open the doors to success for you.

In the Bible, such responsible people are said to have "favor" with their leaders. Daniel, Nehemiah, Esther, and many others found favor with their leaders, even when those leaders were pagan, evil people. How did they do it? They showed themselves responsible. They did the right thing.

By contrast, there are three types of followers who just don't "get it" about the importance of good followership (avoid being like them!):

- **Lazy Lucas.** Lucas moves in slow motion. It's as if he can't awaken from his slumber long enough to carry out his assignment.

- **Irresponsible Irene.** Irene's "poor me" attitude leads her to blame others and become bitter when the leader doesn't cater to her needs.

- **Insincere Ivan.** Instead of talking softly and carrying a big stick, Ivan blusters loudly and carries a twig. He never seems to fulfill his grand promises.

(2) Flee the integrity killers. To have integrity means that you'll be honest and above board in your dealings with others. Want to be a follower with integrity? Be sincere, gracious,

[handwritten margin note: Or are you like these people?]

[handwritten margin note: → Makes promises but never keep them.]

and responsible. And never, ever participate in these three integrity-killers:

• **Back-stabbing.** One of our company's customers loves to gossip by "sharing concerns" with me. This person frequently "goes off" on other people—many of whom are friends of mine. It makes me extremely uncomfortable, and I've tried to address the issue. It's hard to fully trust back-stabbers because anyone who talks to a back-stabber always wonders, "What do they say about *me* when *I'm* not around?"

• **Breaking the chain of command.** As a recent college graduate, I began directing a project that involved, among other things, working with a gifted young speaker. During a minor disagreement, the young man cut off our conversation and sent a nasty fax to my boss, demanding that I be fired. I was hurt by the fact that the young man tried to pull strings rather than talk to me personally about it. My boss supported me, and I tried to respond gracefully by working through the problem and keeping the young man on the project. However, I stopped recommending him as a speaker—I couldn't imagine inflicting him on anyone else.

• **Betraying loyalty.** The Bible tells of a servant who begged his master to forgive him an enormous debt.

The master complied, but the servant immediately went to one of his own servants and viciously demanded payment of a small sum. Upon hearing this, the master was incensed, promptly revoked his pardon, and tossed the disloyal servant into debtor's prison. Many leaders make tremendous personal investments in the lives of their followers. If followers repay them by abandoning them or failing to represent their interests, those followers shouldn't be surprised to find themselves treated with contempt.

Followership Principle #2: Make the Boss Successful.

I used to assume that everyone knew this principle. Imagine my surprise when I discovered that the vast majority of people remain clueless about why their boss won't promote them and why they're always the first to go when downsizing hits.

Here's the secret most have missed: *Work so as to be indispensable.* Being indispensable means you're such a valuable part of the team that the boss would be foolish to let you go.

How can you become this kind of follower? It begins with this simple, blunt understanding: Leaders are interested in you because you can help them advance toward their goals. If you're more trouble than you're worth,

> "Insistence on security is incompatible with the way of the cross...to follow Jesus is always to accept at least a measure of uncertainty, danger and rejection for his sake."[1]
>
> —John R. Stott

How to Make a Persuasive Appeal

How can you apply godly persuasion in your life? First, make sure you've been responsible and that you understand the person you're attempting to influence. Then follow these tips to help make your message more palatable:

• Write in one sentence the essence of what you want to convey.

• Write down in specific terms exactly what you want the leader to do.

• Write down the reasons for acting. Focus only on the reasons you believe the leader will find persuasive.

• Be aware of the reasons against acting as you suggest, and be prepared to explain why you think action is justified. You'll gain credibility by saying, "There is a downside to what I am suggesting. Here is how I would respond to it."

• Be prepared to discuss an alternative. "If 'X' is not possible, maybe we could take a smaller step in the same direction by doing 'Y'."

they'll shoot you off your horse as soon as they can draw a gun.

How can you know whether you're more trouble than you're worth? Here are some key indicators that you might be: failing to anticipate problems, trying to pass your problems on to the boss, thinking every problem is urgent (or conversely, every problem is "no big deal"), and focusing on your own needs first.

Good followers anticipate possible problems and develop contingency plans. Folks who appear to be "quick thinking" in a crisis are simply the ones who thought in advance about how to handle problems that might arise.

In addition, good followers take responsibility for problems. Most bosses get tired of employees "putting the monkey on their back." Instead of weighing your boss down with more problems, bring the problem and two or three possible solutions that you are willing to take responsibility for implementing. You'll be a refreshment for your boss, and he or she won't forget it.

Finally, good followers are loyal. If your intent is to make your boss successful, you will be appreciated, and others in authority positions will notice. Loyalty does not mean always agreeing with the boss, though. Sometimes being loyal means creatively confronting the boss to help him or her make good decisions. But loyalty makes you an indispensable part of the team and *that* places you on the track to leadership and responsibility.

(1) Don't do as the Vulcans do. Since being a good follower doesn't always mean doing what the leader says without question, you will face times when you must try to persuade the leader to do something differently. How can you do this with grace and style?

When helping Jessica with her speech, I said, "All throughout Scripture, God used the unredeemed motives of unbelievers to accomplish His purposes. Get a sense of what your professor considers important, and use that as the basis for your speech."

Sometimes I think it would be nice to do, like Mr. Spock on the old *Star Trek* show, a "Vulcan mind-meld" to download my thoughts. In the end, though, persuasion is a much better method because it involves two minds rather than one. To be persuasive with your authorities, you must demonstrate that doing what you want will help them achieve their goals and motivations. You may not be able to change the mind of the leader, but you can create respect for your position. In time, this can lead to genuine persuasion.

Practice this principle right now by thinking of a person you would like to persuade. Invest five minutes or so following the steps in the "Persuasive Appeal" sidebar on page 76 to craft a persuasive message you can actually use in a situation you're facing right now.

The Bible contains stories of many leaders who responded to their authorities in this way. In Luke 7, Jesus entered the city of Capernaum and was told that a Roman centurion—a military leader in charge of 100 men—had a sick servant. As Jesus approached his home, the man sent out a representative to say:

Lord, don't trouble Yourself, since I am not worthy to have You come under my roof. That is why I didn't even consider myself worthy to come to You. But say the word, and my servant will be cured. For I too am a man placed under authority, having soldiers under my command. I say to this one, 'Go!' and he goes; and to another, 'Come!' and he comes; and to my slave, 'Do this!' and he does it. (Luke 7:6-8)[1]

When Jesus heard this, the Bible says He was amazed and commented to the crowd following Him, "I tell you, I have not found so great a faith even in Israel" (Luke 7:9).

This centurion understood power and leadership. As a man in a position of authority, he was also *under* authority. He recognized that the same was true with Jesus: Jesus had been given authority by the Father to heal sin and disease. The centurion used the authority he had been given to go to

bat for his followers, just as Jesus had done. This principle of authority is so profound that Jesus commended the centurion's approach as the greatest act of faith He had seen in Israel.

Those who demonstrate integrity under authority are most likely to understand and use authority properly. Here are some techniques that will help you pull it off:

(2) Recognize that the leader is not like you. Your leader likely doesn't see the world the same as you do. He has developed his leadership approach based on motivations and reasons you cannot understand unless you put yourself in his place. It's okay to have differences—differences can be good. But if you let personality issues and stereotypes dictate how you interact with leaders, you'll miss the opportunity to have a positive influence on them.

If you find yourself wanting to express views that are different from the leader's views, you can say, "I know you have a lot of reasons why you're planning to take the course of action you've suggested, and I'd like to help you reach your goals. I've been thinking of a way that would help us be even more successful in reaching our goals, and I'd like to present it to you if you're interested."

(3) Recognize what you have in common with the leader. "There may be a surprising number of things you have in common with your professor and classmates," I told Jessica, as she prepared her second speech on sin. "They may not like to talk about 'sin,' but most people know that they do things which violate their intuitive sense of right and wrong. Most people know that some of the things happening in our world are not right. Use this sense to help make room for your position."

All people have internal motivations for why they do what they do. While these differ depending on their situation in life, it's safe to say that all leaders are concerned about at least three things: unity, order, and progress. *Unity* means that people work together in harmony. *Order* is the opposite of chaos–getting the work done in a timely fashion and in a quality manner. *Progress* means growing financially, in reputation, or in reaching goals.

Can you see how these motivations play into your own life? You want to get along with others. You want to move away from chaos and toward order. You want to see progress toward your goals. If you can find a way to appeal to these motives in your leader, you'll dramatically increase your success as a follower.

(4) Take the leader's interests into account. Why do people do what they do? What drives them to act? Effective followers always frame their message in terms that the leader can relate to.

For instance, no competent car salesperson would try to get you to buy a car with, "Please buy this car because I will get a huge commission." No! Instead, he tries to discover what you want in a car, knowing that if you find one that fits your criteria, you'll be significantly more likely to buy.

Common sense, you say? Unfortunately, most people fail in persuasion because they are too self-centered to consider the needs, desires, and motivations of the person they are trying to persuade.

Followership Principle #3: You May Have to Be a Bit Creative

After we talked, Jessica began plotting her next speech, employing the principles of:

(1) recognizing that her professor is not like her,

(2) discovering what she has in common with her professor, and

(3) taking her professor's interests into account.

I suggested she purchase a copy of Josh McDowell's book, *More Than a Carpenter*, for each of her classmates. Imagine my pleasure when Jessica reported to me that she received an "A" on the speech and that her classmates were actually touched by her simple, yet potentially life-changing gift. "It cost me a lot of money, but it was worth it many times over for the impact it had on the class," she said.

One of the best examples of creativity is found in the life of Daniel, a Judean who was taken captive in Nebuchadnezzar's siege of Jerusalem and whose story is recounted in the Bible. Through God's favor, Daniel entered the king's personal three-year training program to learn the language and culture of Babylon.

Although he certainly felt honored to be selected, the thought of studying Babylonian culture for three years must have sickened Daniel. It's hard to envision a culture more pagan than that of Babylon. It was a sensuous city, drenched in idol worship, and ruled by Nebuchadnezzar with an iron fist.

In Daniel 1, the Bible explains that part of the king's program involved imbibing the royal food and wine. What a privilege to share the king's own food! Unfortunately, it violated Hebrew dietary laws, so Daniel and his friends would have no part of it. Daniel's refusal terrified the steward in charge. He said, in essence, "If you don't eat this, you'll become weak and ill, and the king will hold me responsible. I'll be a goner."

Daniel and his Judean friends proposed a test: "Give us nothing but vegetables and water for ten days, and then compare us to the other young men." You know the rest of the story—at the end of the ten days, the Judeans looked healthier than the other young men—so much so that the steward put

all of the young men on the Hebrew diet.

Daniel discerned that the king probably didn't care what they ate, only that they become smart, healthy young leaders. By understanding the king's motives, Daniel and his friends simultaneously honored God and avoided making an unnecessary fuss. The lesson? Leaders transcend their circumstances through creative engagement.

So far, we've talked about how to be trustworthy by doing the right thing, making the boss successful, and getting creative. The thing that pulls it all together, though, is *relationship.* That's what we'll talk about next.

Followership Principle #4: Maintain the Relationship

"As tempting as it may be," I told Jessica, "you must not try to subvert God's purposes by 'telling off' your professor or by adopting a defensive, sarcastic attitude in class. At the point of conflict, a *life* speaks louder than a *word.*"

Perhaps you've heard the idea of "burning your bridges." Armies commonly do this when retreating, making it harder for the enemy to chase them. The problem is, once the bridges are burned, they can't go back.

Maybe you're tempted to burn the bridge—tell your leader off and just leave. Don't do it! Try these moves instead:

(continued from previous page, left-hand sidebar)

Wrong: "My boss criticized me in front of someone else and I confronted him angrily, demanding, 'Why did you do that?'"

Right: "I should have made a point to find him at a less stressful time and say, 'I appreciate getting that feedback from you—it helps me improve at my job so that I can be a more productive member of your team. I felt frustrated, though, that it took place in the presence of someone else. I know they felt awkward about it, and I did too. I felt embarrassed and upset. Next time would you pull me aside privately to discuss such things?'"

You may be amazed at how much your display of integrity leaves a positive impression.

> "Man is frequently impatient, and thinks that nothing is doing. But man's time is not God's time....The great Builder makes no mistakes."[2]
>
> —J.C. Ryle

(1) Cast off pretension. "Pretense" means that you have a hidden agenda—that you're trying to hide the truth from your leader by masking your intentions, making excuses, or blaming others. Speak your mind without pretense, and you'll gain credibility. Speak vaguely, blame or accuse others, or employ a whining or complaining tone, and you'll lose credibility.

A few years ago, my secretary walked into my office and said, "May I discuss something important with you for five minutes?" (Notice how she made her request plain and gave me an estimate of how much time it would take–she understood that one of my motivations is to not be trapped in endless conversations!)

She then outlined a business issue she had faced, the decision she had made and the reasons for the decision. She told me, "I believe I made the wrong decision. Here is what I would like to do to correct it, and here is what I will do differently next time."

My respect for this woman skyrocketed because she did not wait for me to find out about the problem. She confronted it directly, took responsibility, and proposed a reasonable course of action.

(2) Practice patience. We can learn something from the advertising industry on this point. The average person must hear about a product or service seven times before they buy. If you "told your customer off" after the first appeal, you would destroy your chances of ever making the sale.

Instead, be patient. If you can't get the big win, try for small gains through time. Cultivate the relationship. Remember, it is ultimately the relationship that will give you credibility and clout, not how you win on any particular issue.

Perhaps you have already burned a few bridges. Why not take a moment right now to write down the names of the people with whom you've done that and determine two specific steps you will take to rebuild the relationship?

Yes, But What if My Leader Is *Preventing* My Success?

In an ideal world, being a good follower would guarantee leadership success. Unfortunately, reality doesn't work that way. You may find yourself under the authority of a leader who has no vision for your success—or worse, wants you to succeed at the wrong thing.

As a high school student, a lot of people told me I should be a lawyer (my mother was one of them, but I think she suggested it during one of my more quarrelsome moments). Amazingly, I didn't really look into what it would be like to be a lawyer.

I didn't take the time to study what lawyers *do*. I just went to college and majored in political science.

And...I hated it—especially the classes that dealt with *law*! What I really *loved* was communication, so I added a communication studies major and changed direction. I can easily see, however, that if the expectations of others had been stronger, I might have stayed the course—even to my own discontent.

I know one man who lived most of his adult life trying to become more financially successful than his father—just to prove the cruel man's dire predictions of failure wrong. And get this: he continued working toward that goal for years after his father had died! Rather than bless his son, that father had cursed him through wrong expectations and put a damper on his son's ultimate success. People face this dilemma in different ways.

One young adult recently said to me, "I would really like to find a career mentor, but my parents disapprove. They think I don't trust them to help me succeed."

Another said, "I'm expected to take over the family business. But it's not what I really love to do. I'm torn."

An assistant pastor said, "Our senior pastor is so dominating that he makes it very difficult for us to flourish in our gifts."

A businessman said, "It seems that I keep getting passed over for promotions. I feel I'm the most qualified, but all I get is rejection, rejection, rejection. I don't know how much longer I can stand it."

Have you ever felt squelched by those in authority over you? Do you sense a gulf between where you are and where you want to be? The world's response is, "Forget everyone else—follow your dreams." Yet deep inside we know this selfish approach doesn't lead to true satisfaction. Nor does it provide the opportunities for growth God wants to bring into our lives.

Very often God gives us a glimpse of an exciting vision, but other people in our lives don't understand or go along with that vision. How do we deal with that? How do we decide whether or not these expectations are legitimate—and if they aren't legitimate, how do we confront them in an honorable way?

What Do They Want From Me Anyway?

It is right and good that our authorities have certain expectations of us. Expectations can be powerful tools to develop the character we need in order to glorify God. Sometimes, however, these expectations can be expressed in a way that diminishes our calling. If we respond in a rebellious fashion, it can damage the relationship and hamper God's blessing in our lives.

Here are four questions to guide you in how to handle the expectations of others in an honorable, gracious way:

> "The Lord's slave must not quarrel, but must be gentle to everyone, able to teach, and patient, instructing his opponents with gentleness. Perhaps God will grant them repentance to know the truth. Then they may come to their senses and escape the Devil's trap, having been captured by him to do his will."
>
> —2 Timothy 2:24-26

Expectation Question #1: What character qualities does God want to develop in my life?

Discern the character development that needs to take place. Often others' expectations of us are based on legitimate concerns. They may see flaws in us that we can't see in ourselves: a spirit of laziness, rebellion against authority, an unwillingness to risk failure, or a desire to avoid responsibility. One of the main reasons authority figures are resistant to our plans is that they see how our lack of character could cause us to fail.

One young man asked me for counsel about vocational issues and expressed concern that his father was not pleased with his choices. "I want to do 'X,' but he just wants me to get a job in his business and learn to work hard." In looking further into the issue, I learned that the father felt the young man lacked the character quality of perseverance. He was legitimately concerned that his son would fail in his career choice because he wasn't willing to work hard at it.

Expectation Question #2: Am I committed to the leader's success?

Make sure you are communicating the right thing in the right way. Let's say you're an only child, and you select a college a long way away from home. Regardless of how rational your choice, the symbolism to your mother might be, "I'm trying to get away from you." You'll need to invest a lot of time and loving comfort in demonstrating the effort you'll make to stay close emotionally even while apart.

Expectation Question #3: Am I demonstrating honor?

All authorities are due honor—even ungodly ones. Noah Webster's 1828 dictionary defines "honor" this way: "To revere; to respect; to treat with deference and submission, and perform relative duties to." Notice the criterion for honor is not that we *feel* we are being honorable, but that we are *acting* in an honorable way. It's worth pondering, "What specifically can I *do* to demonstrate that I honor this person?"

Many times our attitude or approach creates an impression of dishonor. If someone says, "You don't respect me," ask, "What specific things have I done that demonstrate disrespect?" They may mention something trivial, but that's okay—smaller things are easier to fix!

Expectation Question #4: Have I communicated my vision clearly?

I have found that I often communicate my vision very well to total strangers and not clearly at all to those close to home—those at my church, at work, and my neighbors.

If they don't understand my vision, it doesn't make any sense to them that

I'm running all over the country speaking, writing, and so forth. When I *do* explain it clearly, however, I gain new allies and prayer partners—even among those who might have been suspicious before.

If it's an issue of a vision God has given you and you're unsure of how others will respond, consider having a heart-to-heart talk. You might be surprised at a leader's level of support.

All in Good Time

Galatians 6:9 says, "So we must not get tired of doing good, for we will reap at the proper time if we don't give up." Honor God, and He will exalt you in His good timing. He—the almighty, sovereign Lord—knows best the precise moment at which our gifts and passions will make the greatest difference for His kingdom. If we lose that sense of God's timing we may try to exalt ourselves and, like the man at the banquet who prematurely took his place at the head table, we'll be cast down and humiliated. It's a whole lot better to take the lower place and be called by God to step forward!

A number of years ago, I was working in a leadership position for a Christian ministry. I had a strong desire to go to school to work toward my doctoral degree, but I didn't have the time or money to pull it off.

For one full year I languished. I couldn't save any money because I was essentially working for room, board,

and a small stipend. Furthermore, I was working sixteen hours a day and facing several frustrating challenges. Many times I wanted to quit, but instead I dived into my work, seeking to make the leader of the ministry successful by developing the curricula materials, and programs that would expand his vision.

After a year of pouring my life into the organization, I had a heart-to-heart talk with the director, expressing my desire to work toward my doctorate and indicating how I thought it might help the organization reach its goals.

The leader didn't think much of the idea. "How can we get everything done if you're off at school?" I left deeply disappointed but chose to stick with the job. Within one month of that conversation, and completely unexpectedly, the director gave me the opportunity to lead a massive curriculum development project. That project, *Understanding the Times*, opened doors for speaking and writing I could never have opened for myself. Much of my professional reputation today comes from having excelled on that project.

In addition, when the project was complete, the leader of the organization actually encouraged me to begin work on my doctorate. In fact, he gave me time off to get the degree, increased my salary, and even paid thousands of dollars of my tuition!

In *my* timing, I would have resigned my job and gone off to school. But I would have missed all of the phenomenal opportunities that form the basis of the ministry I have today. It was as if God were saying, "Be patient and wait. In My timing I'll bless you more than you could ever imagine."

Does it always work out so nicely? Of course not. But would you rather obey God and have Him be your advocate, or go it alone?

Time to Get Out There and ...

The more our culture becomes hostile to Christianity, the more we must seek to become excellent leaders. That means we also have to become outstanding followers—standing for truth in a persuasive and loving way.

The Bible assures us that we live in the midst of spiritual war and that we are to be dressed and ready for battle (Ephesians 6:10-18), what the Marines call "locked and loaded." Rather than killing or capturing our enemy, however, the goal in a spiritual war is to *set the captives free* from Satan's trap by helping them come to know the truth.

We can only be successful in this cause by following the example of Jesus Christ and earning the right to be heard (2 Timothy 2:24-26).

Now get out there and follow!

Notes

1. John R. Stott, *The Cross of Christ* (Downers Grove, IL: InterVarsity Press, 1986), p. 288

2. J.C. Ryle, *Holiness* (Greensboro, NJ: The Homiletic Press, 1956), p. 311.

LET'S TALK ABOUT IT

How would leaders of the organizations you've worked with describe your followership?

Besides Daniel, Esther, and David, can you think of any biblical leaders who won favor because of their excellent followership?

(continued on next page)

(continued from previous page)

Think of three different kinds of authority figures in your life (economic, church, governmental, social, etc.). How can you make each of them more successful?

Dr. Myers suggested discovering what motivates a leader and appealing to those motives when you want to persuade them. What do you think of this idea? How would you do this in a persuasive way rather than a manipulative way?

COACHING TOOL

In Team/Out Team: Measuring Your Followership

Everyone is part of a team, whether it's for work, for sports, at church, or in a community organization. Even being part of a family is like being on a team.

Think of a team in which you invest a lot of time, and answer each question as honestly as you can in relation to how you function on that team. There are no right or wrong answers—just opinions. With each question, record your answer by circling the number which best reflects your opinion, with "1" being "Not at all accurate" and "5" being "Very accurate." Work quickly, putting down the first answer that comes to your mind.

		Not at all accurate				Very accurate
1.	I can always be counted on to do what I say I'm going to do.	1	2	3	4	5
2.	Other people try to tell me what to do, but I tune them out.	1	2	3	4	5
3.	I have a good attitude when I don't agree with a decision that's been made.	1	2	3	4	5
4.	The most important thing is to be true to myself.	1	2	3	4	5
5.	I like to think ahead and solve problems we might face.	1	2	3	4	5
6.	Whether our team succeeds is not my responsibility.	1	2	3	4	5
7.	I enjoy knowing that my success makes my team leader look good.	1	2	3	4	5

(continued on next page)

(continued from previous page)	Not at all accurate			Very accurate	
8. As soon as I find a better opportunity, I'm out of here.	1	2	3	4	5
9. I'm known as a person who stays until the job is done, even if it means staying late.	1	2	3	4	5
10. I dislike being asked to do things that are not my responsibility.	1	2	3	4	5
11. When it comes to working together to achieve our team's goals, people try to get me involved.	1	2	3	4	5
12. I don't care whether people find me easy or difficult to work with.	1	2	3	4	5

(continued on next page)

nued on next page)

(continued from previous page)

Record your response to each question next to that question's number below, then total each column.

Column 1		Column 2	
1.		2.	
3.		4.	
5.		6.	
7.		8.	
9.		10.	
11.		12.	
Total		Total	

If Column 1 is between 18 and 30, you're probably viewed as a good follower. You're more likely to be trusted with responsibility and asked for input. Because you give support and encouragement to others, you're likely to receive encouragement and support yourself.

If Column 2 is between 18 and 30, your followership needs some work. Your teammates probably perceive that you are just there to "put in your time." Unless things change, you'll be denied valuable opportunities to move ahead or have a greater say in the team's direction.

Video Session Six (12 minutes)

• Present the struggle in _____ terms.

• Demonstrate that the _____ is monstrously _____.

• Portray this period of history as _____.

• Emphasize that _____ _____ plays a decisive role.

• Make it _____ to their world.

• Give _____ that lead automatically to _____.

• Convince them that they have the _____

to ensure ultimate _____.

CHAPTER SIX

How to Inspire Dedication in Your Followers

KEY QUOTE

"A vision isn't complete without action.
It doesn't just see what needs to be done.
It perceives how and why to act."

CHAPTER AT A GLANCE

To Accomplish Great Things

Video Coaching Session Summary

• The seven steps to inspiring dedication in your followers.

• How framing your vision in terms of God's global, historic plan will get your team members fired up to accomplish great things.

Dynamic Review

• Little ol' me in a big bad world.

• When the whole world is against you.

• It's not about seeing—it's about perceiving.

• The four stages of vision.

• The secret to moving people to stage four vision.

• Seven principles for inspiring dedication in your followers.

• Seven steps of godly persuasion.

• These principles change everything.

Coaching tool

• Is your group aligned with what is eternally significant? Review these Scriptures to find out.

THE 100-YEAR PERIOD BETWEEN 1750 AND 1850 has been called the greatest century of missions. During that time, hundreds of brave missionaries overcame withering criticism and crippling societal indifference to reach out to a world rife with disease, barbarism, cannibalism, and slavery. They faced tremendous persecution, heartache and death, all in the cause of spreading the Christian gospel.

It is easy to forget just how brutal life was for most people on earth just 150 years ago. When John Paton went to New Hebrides, for example, it was common practice for a man to kill his best wife and serve her as the main course at a feast. Infanticide and other unspeakable evils were the norm.

Missionary pioneers such as William Carey, David Livingstone, Mary Slessor, Hudson Taylor, and John Paton were leaders in the finest sense of the word. They envisioned what they wanted to accomplish, they created lasting change, and they inspired others.

Today these missionaries might be criticized for "imposing their morality" on other cultures. But there is no disputing the fact that their civilizing influence brought liberty, peace, health, prosperity, and spiritual well-being to hundreds of millions of people.

Little Ol' Me in a Big Bad World

Can you imagine how utterly intimidating it would be to sail off alone into the unknown, desiring to serve King Jesus fully and completely, but knowing that in all likelihood you would die a horrible death before reaching a single convert?

Maybe your cause isn't so grand, but you still feel the way those brave Christian adventurers felt: small, powerless, despised, and seemingly destined to lose. Maybe you're afraid people will see you as hopelessly unrealistic or worse, ill-equipped for the task to which you have been called. Do you long to see things change…to see people change…to inspire a new level of deep commitment to the cause?

If so, you're poised for a breakthrough. The same scriptural principles that roused the missionary pioneers to action are available to you today. They still can inspire tremendous dedication in your own organization. In this chapter, you'll learn how to frame your vision in a way that creates insatiable curiosity and rock-solid loyalty to your cause.

When the Whole World Is Against You

William Wilberforce was the member of Parliament whose efforts led to the abolition of the British slave trade. He started his campaign of opposition in 1789 at age 30 and slogged away at it for nearly twenty years, enduring fierce hostility until legislation that banned the slave trade finally passed in 1807.

During those two decades, Wilberforce fought political corruption, promoted Christian morality in society, established a colony for freed slaves (Sierra Leone), and forced the British East India Company to allow missionaries so a whole generation could follow after William Carey. No one was more involved than Wilberforce—during his career he was the president, vice-president, or a member of 69 compassion societies!

And he didn't stop after achieving his initial goal. Once Britain abolished the slave trade, Wilberforce set about freeing the 700,000 slaves remaining in British colonies. He succeeded in 1833, just three days before his death.

William Wilberforce was one of the most influential men of his day, in spite of frequent illness and vicious mockery. His tomb in Westminster

Abbey says it best: "He was among the foremost of those who fixed the character of their times..."[1]

But Wilberforce is one of the most influential men of *our* day as well. Momentum from his work in Britain led to the abolition of slavery in America and opened the continent of Africa to missionary influence. Revivals in Africa and in South America lead experts to conclude that these two continents will be the new centers of Christian spirituality within two generations. It's not just a "form" of Christianity either —it's the evangelistic, conservative kind that brought about the Reformation and the Great Awakening. Philip Jenkins, in his book, *The Next Christendom*, explains that "The churches that have made most dramatic progress in the global South have either been Roman Catholic, of a traditionalist and fideistic kind, or radical Protestant sects, evangelical, or Pentecostal."[2]

So great is the spiritual fervor in those places, and so great is the spiritual poverty in the West, that African, Asian, and South American missionaries are now descending on the United States and Great Britain! It's ironic, but what a testimony it is to the enduring legacy of those original missionary pioneers. It took more than 100 years for their efforts to germinate, but once they did, the abundance of fruit promised great hope for the future.

It's Not About Seeing—It's About Perceiving

Dan Egeler points out in *Mentoring Millennials* that to move toward action people must:

- Believe what they know;

- Value what they believe;

- Internalize what they believe; and

- Appropriately act on what they believe.[4]

You can't really say you know the truth until you begin acting on it. There must be a bridge between knowing and doing, between vision and action.

Sadly, most people never cross that bridge. They know the truth, or a form of it, but it has no effect on their lives. They see, but they cannot perceive. They look at things, but they don't notice what is important from God's perspective.

There's a fascinating bit of research that explains the gulf between knowing the truth and acting on it. Some years ago, Russian scientists developed a surgical technique which restored sight to people who had previously been blind. In examining the newly seeing patients, the researchers discovered something shocking.

The patients were blindfolded and asked to feel the shape and texture of an apple and an orange. The blindfolds were then removed, and the patients asked to distinguish the difference be-

> "Jesus boldly promised, 'I will build My church, and the gates of Hades shall not prevail against it.' ... we are to be advancing against, not retreating from, hell's gates. In the end, they will not be able to withstand the Lord of hosts' attack."[3]
>
> —Rice Broocks

tween the two fruits by sight. Imagine the researchers' surprise when they discovered that the patients failed this test. While these newly sighted people could feel the differences in texture and shape, they had no experience at relating what they felt to what they saw. In other words, they could see, but they could not perceive.

A vision isn't complete without action. It doesn't just see what needs to be done, it perceives how and why to act, in full view of the threats and opportunities inherent in the situation. How can you bridge the gap between vision and action for your group? That's what we'll examine next.

The Four Stages of Vision

In my years of studying leadership, I've become convinced there are four stages through which a person moves from seeing to perceiving. I call these the "four stages of vision":

Stage 1—Notice the problem.
Vision-driven leaders notice things. They actually take in more information when looking at the same things everyone else sees.

Stage 2—Sense the urgency.
Vision-driven leaders feel it in the gut. They know what's important and cannot remain passive about it.

Stage 3—Anticipate involvement.
Vision-driven leaders take it personally. They cannot rest until they find

a role that allows them to take constructive action.

Stage 4—Commit to action.
Vision-driven leaders never passively accept what is in their power to change. They desire to make a difference everywhere.[5]

Most people can attain Stage 1 vision very easily by listening to a speaker, viewing a television newscast or hearing scuttlebutt from a friend. A significantly smaller percentage move to Stage 2 by sensing that "Something must be done." An even smaller percentage moves on to Stage 3, wondering, "What should I do? What's my part?" Ultimately, only a tiny fraction of the Stage 1 visionaries move all the way through to Stage 4, committing to action.

This process of moving from Stage 1 to Stage 4 vision can be seen clearly in the life of a biblical character, Gideon, from the book of Judges.

Gideon's Stage Four Leaders

The story of Gideon's army, recorded in Judges 6, provides an eye-opening illustration of the transition from Stage 1 through Stage 4 vision. The story goes like this: although Gideon claimed to be the weakest member of the weakest tribe of Israel, God called him to lead an army to defeat the Midianites who were ravaging the Israelites' land year after year.

Arguably, all of the Israelites had Stage 1 vision. They knew what the problem was: they suffered bitterly at the hands of the Midianites. When called to fight, however, only 32,000 moved to Stage 2. They sensed the urgency of the cause and chose to join the army. When Gideon released those who were too afraid to fight, though, he discovered that only 10,000 were willing to move to Stage 3. These few knew that only their personal involvement would rid them of the Midianite plague.

Out of these 10,000 with Stage 3 vision, God selected only 300. The Bible says they were chosen because they lapped up water with their hands rather than getting down on their knees to drink. No one knows why God chose this selection criterion. It's possible that the ones who remained on their feet were seen as the most committed to action. In any event, only 300 men made it to Stage 4.

We could picture it like this:

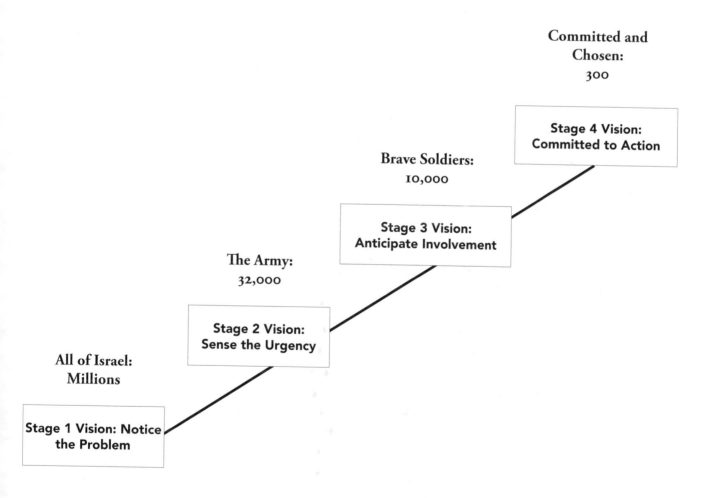

Committed and
Chosen:
300

**Stage 4 Vision:
Committed to Action**

Brave Soldiers:
10,000

**Stage 3 Vision:
Anticipate Involvement**

The Army:
32,000

**Stage 2 Vision:
Sense the Urgency**

All of Israel:
Millions

**Stage 1 Vision: Notice
the Problem**

> "Leadership is not so much the exercise of power itself as the empowerment of others."[6]
>
> —Warren Bennis and Burt Nanus

Think of it. The 300 committed and chosen soldiers were a tiny fraction of the population. In fact, they constituted less than one percent of those who knew that something needed to be done right away. Yet God led them to overwhelming victory.

The moral of the story? True vision is rare—only a few ever get it, but the impact, in God's hands, is awesome.

Is there a secret to increasing the percentage of those in your organization who have Stage 4 vision? I believe there is, and it's not what you would expect.

The Secret to Moving People to Stage Four Vision

What would cause a group of people to make dramatic sacrifices for an uncertain and dangerous cause? The great missionary pioneers seemed to understand it. However, most folks I've met doubt whether they have the personal power to move people to dedicated action. Is it actually possible for an everyday leader to awaken people to their God-given potential and move them to victorious action? Emphatically, yes.

I'm convinced that the bridge between vision and action is *inspiration*. "Inspire" means to "breathe life into; any stimulus to creative thought or action." Inspiration is vastly superior to motivation. Where the motivated person takes action in hopes of personal gain, the inspired person breathes in the vision until it becomes a deep source of life energy. The inspired person can no more remain passive than he can will his heart to stop beating.

Inspired leaders dive in—seeking ways to live more of the life they were meant to live. The highest levels of dedication come through breathing life and enthusiasm into your followers. Inspired leaders achieve success even when the world sees their group as small, powerless, despised and seemingly destined to lose.

To discover how to move from vision to action, from Stage 1 through Stage 4, we need to examine the oddly compelling life of Douglas Hyde.

Seven Principles for Inspiring Dedication in Your Followers

Douglas Hyde was a Communist. In fact, as editor of Great Britain's *Daily Worker* newspaper, he was a Communist *leader*. However, Hyde became disillusioned with Communist doctrine and converted to Catholicism, and the world is a better place because of it for at least one reason: Hyde revealed all of the things that Communists did right.[7]

It's not that Hyde defended Communist doctrine—he found it abhorrent. But his dissection of the Communists' finely tuned recruiting techniques gives us great insight into how to be inspirational leaders.

You see, in Communist countries it was easy to motivate followers. Put a gun to their heads, and they became highly motivated, very quickly. In non-Communist countries, however, it took inspiration. What Hyde revealed about the Communists' "inspiration strategy" was stunning.

When Hyde collected his lectures into a book called *Dedication and Leadership* (published by University of Notre Dame Press and still available today), he rocked the Catholic world by claiming, with numerous persuasive examples, that Communists succeeded because they adopted the biblical discipleship techniques that had been largely abandoned by the church.

In one sense this shouldn't be surprising. Worldviews such as Communism have no good ideas of their own. Whatever they have that works has been begged, borrowed, or stolen from truth-based worldviews. How ironic, though, that Communists were sometimes better at putting truth-based principles into practice than were followers of the truth-based worldviews themselves.

When British Communists wanted to recruit followers and inspire them to be dedicated to the cause, they were under no illusions about the difficulty of their task. The potential Communist thought, "Communists are wrong and evil…people will hate us…we'll surely lose." It would be hard enough to keep members from quitting, let alone to turn them into leaders.

Turn them into leaders they did, however, through a 7-step process.

Seven Steps of Godly Persuasion

The 7-step process through which the British Communists inspired dedi-

cation is an excellent case study of the power of godly persuasion (remember, they commandeered biblical principles).

Step 1—Present the struggle in global terms. Hyde pointed out that no one gets excited about a cause that means very little. If you want people to really sense the significance of what you are doing, show how it fits into "the big picture."

Christians know our world has reached a spiritual flash point. America's Christian heritage has been largely dismantled, and hundreds of millions of people throughout the world suffer hideously within cultural systems based on oppression and lies. As Christopher Dawson, the English intellectual, noted in *Religion and the Rise of Western Culture*:

> Our generation has been forced to realize how fragile and unsubstantial are the barriers that separate civilization from the forces of destruction. We have learned that barbarism is not a picturesque myth or a half-forgotten memory of a long-passed stage of history, but an ugly underlying reality which may erupt with shattering force whenever the moral authority of a civilization loses its control.[8]

We're on the brink of global change. Will change move people closer to God or farther away? Much of the answer depends on how Christians obey

Bringing Vision Down to the Everyday Level

Are your followers apathetic? Maybe they don't catch your vision. They see the same things you see, but they don't perceive the earth-shattering urgency that drives you forward.

Why not develop a series of statements that brings what's important down to an everyday level?

This raises their level of engagement and establishes an organizational culture that prizes inspired action. Here are some statements to consider:

• "In our organization, we don't ignore things. We try to anticipate what is coming down the road and prepare to meet challenges head-on."

(continued on next page)

Christ's command to disciple all nations for Him.

This global struggle is a winner-take-all event.

Step 2—Demonstrate that the enemy is monstrously evil. The "enemy" doesn't have to be a person or a group—it can be a thing. There are a lot of people (especially men, I think) who won't move into action unless there are battles that need to be fought and won.

The spiritual battles of our day are indeed raging, and the more the forces of good appear to prevail, the more evil will rage. This has always been the case. The late Harvard sociologist, Pitirim Sorokin, pointed out that, whenever the world turns toward transcendent truth, the forces of hatred and evil react fiercely:

> My studies led to the generalization that in the great crisis of the transition from the declining old to the new emerging supersystem, the polarization of human souls, groups, and values regularly occurs. ...Some become more saintly, more religious, more ethical; others, more sinful, more atheistic, more cynical than before.[9]

We have no choice except action. Sorokin starkly outlines our options:

> Without the Kingdom of God we are doomed to a weary and torturing pilgrimage from calamity to calamity, from crisis to crisis, with only brief moments of transitory improvement for regaining our breath. In that case the way out will always be the "way of death," ordeal, and destruction.[10]

The enemy is, indeed, monstrously evil.

Step 3—Portray this period of history as decisive. "So the enemy is evil, but how does that affect us, right now?"

You must have a good answer to that question. Why is action at this particular point in time significant?

In many ways, the entire history of Christianity comes down to the age in which we live, not because Christ will return soon—He may or may not—but because we're at a critical point in the history of the West. Secularists—those who oppose America's Christian history or hate what Western Civilization represents—have tremendous influence in the media, the judiciary, and our political system.

What drives these secularists to the brink of madness, however, is their absolute inability to sustain the life of the culture. Secularization has the same effect on a culture that toaster pastries and vodka have when they're all you eat and drink—they seem filling and even pleasurable, but they'll kill you through malnutrition. If history is any measure, secularism's influence will inevitably run its course and collapse from within.

What happens at these moments of decision? We've got to answer that question whether we want to or not. As Richard John Neuhaus says, "The question is not whether the glass is half full or half empty, but what you do when you know it's empty."[11]

You might be surprised by my answer to that moment-of-decision question, because Christianity in the last fifty years has tended toward pessimism about the future. The evidence from history, though, is that when one cultural system dies, another is born to take its place. In other words, it's possible that we are presiding not at the death of Christian history, but at the birth of a new historical epoch based on transcendent truth.

Pitirim Sorokin, the late Harvard sociologist I quoted earlier, had a name for a culture that abandons truth and pursues only its fleshly desires. He called it "Sensate." It's an apt description of the West right now. But in his study of all human civilizations for which we have written records, Sorokin gives a hopeful report:

> My study of the succession of the supersystems during some thirty-five centuries of the Creto-Minoan, Creto-Mycenaean, Greco-Roman, and Western European cultures and in a more cursory way of the Egyptian, Chinese and Hindu cultures has shown likewise that in all observed cases, after the decline of the Sensate supersystem, a new Ideational (religious) supersystem becomes dominant.[12]

And all God's people said, "Huh?" Let me explain. This "ideational super-system" refers to a cultural system that embraces transcendent truth. In short, the old order is collapsing, and in its collapse it presents an opportunity Christians have had only two or three other times in the course of history: to lead the world en masse toward truth.

So, did I mention: This period of history is decisive?

Step 4—Emphasize that each individual plays a decisive role. Not only must the cause be great and the enemy worth opposing, but the importance of acting *now* must be clear to each person because everyone's efforts are crucial.

So what things are really important? We want to provide for and protect our families. We want to better our situations in life. We want freedom to pursue our ideas in a climate of justice and fairness. But what is of *ultimate* importance? Romano Guardini's little book, *The End of the Modern World*, offers a simple yet profound answer to this question. He says, "There is only one standard by which any epoch can be fairly judged: in view of its own peculiar circumstances, to what extent did it allow for the development of human dignity?"[13] In other words, of all of the things that make our lives meaningful, the most important is how our lives serve to build up and nurture others.

I have a question for you. What are you doing that leaves the next generation better off? How are you pushing forward so that those who come behind

---

(continued from previous page)

• "In our organization, passivity is not an option. We will be proactive in handling issues so they don't become problems later on."

• "In our organization, we all take responsibility. We all assume things are our personal responsibility until we find out otherwise."

• "In our organization, everyone has personal gifts and specific roles, but there are times when we all pitch in to do whatever needs to be done."

Use statements like these to show how these principles apply and to give your team permission to hold you accountable to them.

you have a better vantage point from which to build God's kingdom?

When it comes to leaving a legacy, everyone's efforts matter. As Guardini explains,

> [W]e have today an even deeper realization that all existence rests on certain basic forms, and that the individual form is part of a whole, which in turn is affected by the individual. *From this springs the awareness that everything affects everything.* [emphasis mine][14]

In other words, every one of us plays a decisive role.

Step 5—Make it meaningful to their world. Persuasion researcher Leon Festinger coined the term "cognitive dissonance" to describe the difference between where people are and where they know they ought to be. To inspire your followers, you've got to throw a wrench in the gears, showing that to go on as before would be to live inconsistently with what they believe.

At this critical moment in history, God has raised up a generation that hungers for Him. It has experienced the worst of what secularism has to offer and is ready for change. Wendy Murray Zoba expands on this theme in *Generation 2K*:

> Moral ambiguity has spurred [Millennials] to want decisive boundaries and real answers. Spiritual longing has made them ready to give it everything they've got in their quest

for God. In other words, they will do things in the extreme. When they answer the call to heroism, they will answer it boldly. When it comes to embracing moral truth, they will do so unabashedly. When they give their lives to the Lord, they will serve with everything on the line.[15]

There was never a better time, and we have a generation bursting with potential to build God's kingdom. This cause gives meaning to every life on planet Earth.

Step 6—Give instruction that leads automatically to action. As a graduate student at Baylor University, I studied the self-defeating rhetoric of environmental extremism. Many of the "tree huggers" of that day, such as Jeremy Rifkin, were producing frightening tomes detailing apocalyptic scenarios of environmental destruction.[16] The theme seemed to be, "The world is falling apart, and there is nothing we can do to stop it, so act now." Why should you act when you know for certain that your actions will not have the slightest effect on the outcome? I still chuckle when I recall how many of those radicals actually seemed puzzled by the fact that no one found their rhetoric motivating.

If you want action, you must show that action will be fruitful. If Rifkin and company had hired me as their communication consultant, I would have encouraged them to spread the message that, "This problem is *almost* unsolvable, except that there are people like us, who have 'X' going for us. So let's act right away."

The "ask" is the heart of every persuasive message. If you properly construct your message, people will want to respond. Therefore, you must give them a clear way to act.

The course of action for Christians is clear—we must learn how to live out our entire worldview in a compelling and practical way. Sorokin explains:

[T]he revival of this [transcendent] ethic needs a corresponding "philosophy" or "world-view"…based not only upon a purely rational or sensory basis, but…unifying in itself the intuitive, the rational, and the sensory "evidence" of its validity and practical effectiveness.[17]

It's time to cultivate the habit of giving instruction that leads automatically to action.

Step 7—Convince them that they have the means to ensure ultimate victory. Step 7 is the key to long-term success. Being convinced that, whatever happens, we will win in the end is vital to a group's ability to withstand the pressures that come with creating change.

Is it possible that a small number of enlightened people can actually have a massive influence on the world? Yes, but don't take my word for it. University of Pennsylvania professor Randall Collins' enormous book, *The Sociology of Philosophies*, documents—in more than a thousand pages of diagrams,

explanations, and footnotes—exactly how each civilization in history was shaped by a handful of individuals who took the time to think through the abstract, theoretical principles undergirding their worldviews.

Collins details the characteristics of these super-influencers:

• They are very few in number—as few as 150 and no more than 3,000.

• They work with abstract ideas that seem to bear no relationship to everyday life.

• They operate in networks of like-minded individuals who mentor others.

• They have the emotional energy to develop cultural capital (symbols that can be acted upon).

• They develop their ideas in the context of opposition.[18]

Small, determined groups of super-influencers appear to be inconsequential to their contemporaries. The course of history proves that ordinary people acting purposefully have an extraordinary influence. Here's how Collins phrases it:

I am arguing that if one can understand the principles that determine intellectual networks, one has a causal explanation of ideas and their changes….The history of philosophy is to a considerable extent the history of groups. Nothing abstract is meant here—nothing but groups of friends, discussion partners, close-knit circles that often have the characteristics of social movements.[19]

Never underestimate the power of determined people working in small groups toward a well-defined goal. University of Notre Dame scientist Albert-László Barabási uses the example of the Apostle Paul to describe the power of such an approach:

> [Paul] used his firsthand knowledge of the social network of the first century's civilized world from Rome to Jerusalem to reach and convert as many people as he could. He walked nearly 10,000 miles in the next twelve years of his life. He did not wander randomly, however; he reached out to the biggest communities of his era, to the people and places in which the faith could germinate and spread most effectively. He was the first and by far the most effective sales person of Christianity; using theology and social networks equally effectively.[20]

Perhaps you feel that your life doesn't really matter in the grand scheme of things. The historians, philosophers, and sociologists of our day have proven otherwise: *what you do really matters*. As literary genius Jorge Luis Borges reflected, "Everything touches everything."[21]

Your very own hands provide the ultimate means of victory.

These Principles Change Everything

These seven principles are revolutionary in moving people from vision to action.

One final point: teaching these seven inspiration principles is not just a one-time gig. Expound on them repeatedly in many ways, and live them out faithfully in full view of your group members. Be on the lookout for new evidence that proves that what you do matters, and make sure members of your group see their individual contributions with dazzling clarity!

Notes

1. Information about William Wilberforce may be found in Peter Hammond, *The Greatest Century of Missions* (Cape Town, SA: Christian Action, 2003).

2. Philip Jenkins, *The Next Christendom: The Coming of Global Christianity* (New York: Oxford University Press, 2002), p. 7.

3. Rice Broocks, *Every Nation in Our Generation* (Lake Mary, FL: Creation House, 2002), p. 19.

4. Dan Egeler, *Mentoring Millennials: Shaping the Next Generation* (Colorado Springs, CO: NavPress, 2003), p. 71.

5. Based on Jeff Myers, *Secrts of the World-Changers* (Dayton, TN: Myers Institute, 1997).

6. Warren Bennis and Burt Nanus, *Leaders: The Strategies for Taking Charge* (New York: Haper and Row, 1985).

7. Douglas Hyde, *Dedcation and Leadership* (South Bend, IN: Unversity of Notre Dame Press, 1987)

8. Christopher Dawson, *Religion and the Rise of Western Culture* (New York: Doubleday, 1950), p. 24.

9. Pitirim Sorokin, *Social Philosophies in an Age of Crisis*, 1970, p. 297.

10. Pitirim Sorokin, *Man and Society in Calamity* (New York: E. P. Dutton, 1942), p. 319

11. Introduction to *The End of the Modern World* (Wilmington, DE: ISI Books, 1998), p. x.

12. *Social Philosophies in an Age of Crisis*, p. 294.

13. *The End of the Modern World*, p. 23.

14. *The End of the Modern World*, p. 185.

15. *Generation 2K: What Parents and Others Need to Know About the Millennials* (Downers Grove, IL: InterVarsity Press, 1999), p. 64.

16. See especially Rifkin, *Entropy* (New York: Bantam Books, 1980).

17. *Social Philosophies in an Age of Crisis*, p. 294.

18. Summary of Randall Collins' conclusions throughout *The Sociology of Philosophies* (Cambridge, MA: Harvard University Press, 1998).

19. Collins, *The Sociology of Philosophies*, pp. xviii, 3.

20. Albert-László Barabási, *Linked* (Cambridge, MA: Perseus Publishing, 2002), p. 4.

21. Quoted in Barabási, p. 5.

LET'S TALK ABOUT IT

Think of an organization that has a higher than average number of "Stage 4" (committed to action) leaders. What sets this organization apart? What can you learn from this organization to apply to your own group?

How is this period of history decisive for your group? Why is it important that you act now to accomplish your goals? How might this be communicated vividly to your group?

(continued on next page)

(continued from previous page)

Dr. Myers said, "You can't really say you know the truth until you begin acting on it. There must be a bridge between knowing and doing, between vision and action." Do you agree or disagree? What could be done in your own group to move people to action?

Coaching Tool

If you knew that your life were ending, what would you say to communicate a vision to someone in whom you had invested your life? That's exactly what the Apostle Paul's letter called 2 Timothy is. It's Paul's final word. He's about to die and go to heaven, and he wants to make sure Timothy stays strong in spite of hardship.

With each verse or passage below, write down the key point that relates to what you've been learning about communicating a vision.

For example:

1:3—"I thank God, whom I serve with a clear conscience as my forefathers did, when I constantly remember you in my prayers night and day."	Pray constantly!

Your turn:

1:6—"Therefore, I remind you to keep ablaze the gift of God that is in you through the laying on of my hands"	
1:7—"For God has not given us a spirit of fearfulness, but one of power, love, and sound judgment."	
1:8—"So don't be ashamed of the testimony about our Lord, or of me His prisoner. Instead, share in suffering for the gospel, relying on the power of God…"	
1:12b—"But I am not ashamed, because I know whom I have believed and am persuaded that He is able to guard what has been entrusted to me until that day."	

(continued on next page)

(continued from previous page)

2:2—"And what you have heard from me in the presence of many witnesses, commit to faithful men who will be able to teach others also."	
2:3-5—"Share in suffering as a good soldier of Christ Jesus. To please the recruiter, no one serving as a soldier gets entangled in the concerns of everyday life. Also, if anyone competes as an athlete, he is not crowned unless he competes according to the rules."	
2:8—"Keep in mind Jesus Christ, risen from the dead, descended from David, according to my gospel."	
2:14—"Remind them of these things, charging them before God not to fight about words; this is in no way profitable and leads to the ruin of the hearers."	
2:15-16—"Be diligent to present yourself approved to God, a worker who doesn't need to be ashamed, correctly teaching the word of truth. But avoid irreverent, empty speech, for this will produce an even greater measure of godlessness."	

(continued on next page)

(continued from previous page)

2:22—"Flee from youthful passions, and pursue righteousness, faith, love, and peace, along with those who call on the Lord from a pure heart."	
2:23-26—"But reject foolish and ignorant disputes, knowing that they breed quarrels. The Lord's slave must not quarrel, but must be gentle to everyone, able to teach, and patient, instructing his opponents with gentleness. Perhaps God will grant them repentance to know the truth. Then they may come to their senses and escape the Devil's trap, having been captured by him to do his will."	
3:1-5—"But know this: difficult times will come in the last days. For people will be lovers of self, lovers of money, boastful, proud, blasphemers, disobedient to parents, ungrateful, unholy, unloving, irreconcilable, slanderers, without self-control, brutal, without love for what is good, traitors, reckless, conceited, lovers of pleasure rather than lovers of God, holding to the form of religion but denying its power. Avoid these people!"	

(continued on next page)

(continued from previous page)

3:12-14—"In fact, all those who want to live a godly life in Christ Jesus will be persecuted. Evil people and imposters will become worse, deceiving and being deceived. But as for you, continue in what you have learned and firmly believed, knowing those from whom you learned…"

3:16-17—"All Scripture is inspired by God and is profitable for teaching, for rebuking, for correcting, for training in righteousness, so that the man of God may be complete, equipped for every good work."

4:1-5—"Before God and Christ Jesus, who is going to judge the living and the dead, and by His appearing and His kingdom, I solemnly charge you: proclaim the message; persist in it whether convenient or not; rebuke, correct, and encourage with great patience and teaching. For the time will come when they will not tolerate sound doctrine, but according to their own desires, will accumulate teachers for themselves because they have an itch to hear something new. They will turn away from hearing the truth and will turn aside to myths. But as for you. keep a clear head about everything, endure hardship, do the work of an evangelist, fulfill your ministry."

Where Do We Go from Here?

As I SAID IN the introduction, if you're in a formal leadership position, you'll want to dive into DVD lessons (Leadership Solutions 1 through 6) right away. By showing you what to do *now* in your leadership role, they'll build your confidence immensely and give you the tools you need to grow your organization. Even if you're just anticipating taking on an official leadership function sometime in the future, the advanced lessons will prepare you now for what you'll undoubtedly face then. I've also noted below some valuable suggestions no matter what your present role.

After finishing this series you may want to study more on the subject of leadership. I recommend a three-phase process:

Seek to understand the times.

Would you be comfortable following a leader who didn't know what was going on in the world? Of course not. Such a person would be dangerous to follow! You can equip yourself to understand the times from a Christian perspective using the *Thinking Like a Christian* study to make sure you're clear on all the implications of holding to a biblical worldview. Based on the proven strategies of Summit Ministries, this course takes you step by step through the process of developing a confident Christian worldview in theology, philosophy, ethics, biology, psychology, sociology, politics, economics, history, and law.

Unleash your leadership gifts.

Each person has a God-given vision, mission, motivation, and plan—waiting to be unleashed. Use the *Secrets of World Changers* video coaching system to help your group build enthusiasm about what God is doing in and through them.

Conquer fear and communicate with confidence.

The coaching system *Secrets of Great Communicators* makes it simple and fun to design and deliver a great speech. People won't follow a vision unless someone can clearly and persuasively articulate it. This 6-step system shows you what the greatest communicators of all time have done to move people to action.

May the Lord use you mightily as He gives you opportunities to lead others for Him!

APPENDIX ONE

Suggestions for Using This Study in a Group

Lots of different kinds of groups are finding success with *Secrets of Everyday Leaders*. Here are some of the many creative uses:

- Helping Christian school student leaders become equipped with life-long leadership skills.

- Training community leaders to maximize their group's potential.

- Identifying and teaching political action committees the skills of influence and change.

- Coaching church or community group boards to lead their organizations successfully.

- Upbuilding the lives of group volunteers by enhancing their leadership effectiveness.

- Teaching leadership skills to home school co-op, high school, or college students.

- Enhancing your leadership skills at home.

- Training Christian business people and professionals to lead in a God-honoring fashion.

Here's a simple strategy for getting the most out of *Secrets of Everyday Leaders* with your group:

- Begin your meeting by showing the video coaching session (they are between 11 and 22 minutes long).

- Use the discussion questions at the end of the chapter to deepen your group's understanding of the principles.

- Encourage the group to follow up the time together by reading each chapter.

- Show members how to use the coaching tools to plan their individual success—or the group's success—in simple, doable steps.

If you're leading the advanced sessions (Leadership Solutions 1–6, on the DVD only), you'll want to review each one before your meeting and be sure to prepare the handouts provided on the CD-ROM that comes with your DVD package. Take the group step by step through the coaching tools.

9 Strategies for Dynamic Small Groups

Successfully facilitating a study on leadership requires preparation, persistence, and variety. Here are nine simple techniques which will make your group interaction more profitable.

1. Use clear, visible graphics.

You'll almost always benefit by having "tear sheets" or a white board when facilitating a discussion. I prefer Post-it Note® pads that can be torn off and stuck to the wall. These are a valuable tool for brainstorming vision, mission, and strategy. If your group is 10 to 20 members, a marker board or chalkboard will suffice. For groups larger than 20, an overhead projector with acetate sheets works best.

2. Prepare in advance.

Prepare for each session by watching the video and filling in the blanks in the coaching manual (lessons 1-6) or the CD-ROM (Leadership Solutions). This exercise will help you become familiar with the main point of each lesson. Spend a few minutes looking up key passages and jotting down questions and examples which will spark discussion on key points.

3. Ask participants to invest time outside of class.

Emphasize to participants that they will receive a much greater benefit if they faithfully read each chapter and complete the Coaching Tools.

4. Plan for group participation.

When looking up Scripture verses or analyzing discussion questions, ask for input from as many group members as possible. In addition, ask participants to help you by writing responses on the tear sheets during discussions. Be aware, however, that many people are uncomfortable reading aloud or finding Scripture passages on the spur of the moment. Ask for volunteers in advance, assigning passages so they have time to look them up.

5. Foster interaction.

There are many places in each lesson where participants will want to think about and answer questions. Create group interaction by varying the group size and dynamic. Have participants work by themselves or discuss and share in groups of two, three, or four. Groups of more than four are unwieldy, given a limited time frame.

6. Encourage feedback.

Every teacher has experienced days when students are reluctant to contribute. Studies demonstrate, however, that if you ask a clear question and wait, *someone* will invariably respond within 18 seconds, if only to break the silence! Feel free to call on participants for responses, but be aware that some painfully shy individuals feel very uncomfortable sharing. Don't push them too hard. They will open up when they are ready.

7. Keep discussions moving!

A thought-provoking follow-up question can really get a discussion moving, but be careful not to raise questions that cannot be reasonably answered in the allotted amount of time. Also, refrain from arguing with participants about their comments.

8. Corral "aggressive" participants.

Often groups include one or more persons who want to monopolize the conversation. You can usually solve this problem by gently saying something like, "Let's hear from someone else on this question." If the problem is extreme, try pulling the offending person aside after a session to say, "I'm having a hard time getting some of the people in the group to contribute. Since you aren't shy, would you help me encourage others to participate?" This tends to make the person feel valued, and it also gives others the space to contribute.

9. Create variety in small group discussions.

Make small group discussions more stimulating and provide opportunities for practicing leadership skills by varying interaction patterns. One way to do this is by purchasing a variety of stickers commonly available at an office supply store: circles, squares and stars of various colors. As students come into the room, give each of them a sticker, taking care to generate variety. When breaking into groups, have them divide up by the colors and shapes of their stickers (for example, "Get into a group of three with those wearing the same sticker shape you have."). In addition to color or sticker shape, you can divide them by the number you want in each group, by gender, age, eye color, the school they attend(ed), people they haven't spent time with in the previous week, etc. You can select group leaders in the same fashion (i.e., "Get into groups by the shape of your sticker. The person with the color yellow leads the discussion."). Dozens of variations are possible—choose the one that works best for your group.

The Mission and Vision of the Myers Institute

Our mission...
...is to equip generations of culture-shaping
Christians to understand the times, unleash their
God-given gifts, and communicate the truth
with confidence.

Our vision...
...is to equip one million leadership coaches
by the year 2015.

WE EQUIP CHRISTIANS to disciple, mentor and teach the next generation of leaders and assist them to gain positions of significant influence in society. To do this, we develop training resources and programs for culture-shaping leaders to help them coach the next generation of leaders. To accomplish our mission and vision purposes, The Myers Institute follows these action principles:

Passionate commitment to Christ.

The heart of leadership influence is a personal relationship with Christ, which fuels the desire to disciple people to obey God in every area of life.

Biblically measured.

We provide resources and accountability to help culture-shaping leaders be morally pure, sensitive to spiritual things, clear about their God-given design, servant-hearted, and tapped into an excellence-focused team.

Equipped for every good work.

We seek to equip leaders to: become clear about God's design for gender; find freedom from bondage to lust, materialism, or prestige; identify and live out their life's purpose; express reconciliation through a lifestyle of grace; conquer fear and communicate the truth with godly persuasion; discern the conflict of worldviews in our day; integrate work and ministry; become financially generous.

Family centered.

We believe the family is an integral part of God's design for influencing the world. Thus, we focus on: helping singles develop integrity in relationships, encouraging married couples to unite their visions and strengthen their marriages, providing resources for parents to disciple their children, engaging in positive community involvement, adding value to local congregations, and strengthening the effectiveness of the local church.

Reproducing.

Culture-shaping Christians graciously stand for truth in the social arena, boldly share Christ with others, and are faithful to equip future generations.

Leaders who focus on these areas dramatically expand their influence on their families, the world of commerce, the Church, and, ultimately, society.

For more information on the services and ministry of The Myers Institute, check out the organization's website at www.myersinstitute.com.

Recommended Resources

Thinking Like a Christian
David Noebel and Chuck Edwards

This worldview kit harnesses Summit Ministries' 40 years' worth of expertise in teaching world-views—and makes it simple for you to impart to students! The kit includes an easy-to-use teacher guide, CD-ROM, video, student guide, and *Understanding the Times* reference manual.

Countering Culture: Arming Yourself to Confront Non-Biblical Worldviews
David Noebel and Chuck Edwards

This second book in the Worldviews in Focus series equips Christians to take a reasoned stand for biblical principles and to confront opposing worldviews in the classroom as well as in the board-room. The complete set of materials includes a student text, an easy-to-use teacher guide on CD-ROM, and 12 video lessons.

Secrets of the World Changers
Jeff Myers

Find an exciting sense of direction with this biblical approach to gaining a vision, unleashing your God-given gifts, renewing your motivation, and achieving your highest goals. This ground-breaking approach to leadership shows how God can use your gifts, however humble, to have an extraordinary influence on the world.

Secrets of Great Communicators
Jeff Myers

Banish fear and communicate with confidence through this simple system which puts fun into designing and delivering great speeches. *Secrets of Great Communicators* contains 6 video coaching sessions featuring accomplished public speaker Jeff Myers, who reveals the secrets to great communication in a way that you can immediately employ.

For a complete listing of resources offered by the Myers Institute, go to www.myersinstitute.com.

"This is an excellent study. Dr. Myers does a wonderful job of thoroughly explaining how to be an everyday leader while using everyday examples and down-to-earth points. It's wonderfully in-depth, yet you walk away ready to act on what you learned. It's perfect for use as a home school course or for anyone interested in being a leader in everyday life."

Jocelin Boutet, Everyday Leader

"What have I learned from Jeff Myers? You've got to be kidding...there are a multitude of things I've learned through the years, many eye- and mind-openers such as 'Expect God to take you out of your comfort zone' and 'God will ask His children to go one step further...to do big things.' I especially appreciate his focus on 'how to.'"

Sharon Starling, Everyday Leader

"If you want to develop leadership potential in someone else, or if you want to improve your own leadership skills, you should invest in *Secrets of Everyday Leaders*. It's an inspiring, thought-provoking program designed to instill confidence in those of us who think we are just 'ordinary.'"

Tim Butler, Everyday Leader

"Many people operate with self-imposed barriers that prevent them from achieving God's highest purpose for their lives. *Secrets of Everyday Leaders* will help you to recognize those barriers in your own life and to see yourself from God's perspective. It will free you to move forward and make an impact in your world."

Mervin Koehlinger, Everyday Leader

We tend to focus on the charismatic leader and forget that most leaders are ordinary, everyday people who must lead in some capacity. *Secrets of Everyday Leaders* raises the 'everyday leader' to new levels of competence and a greater calling of God in leadership."

Dean Smith, Everyday Leader

"Getting out of your comfort zone can be scary, but *Secrets of Everyday Leaders* proves that it's worth it, and guides you toward becoming a better leader every day. You can start now, no matter where you are in life!"

Randall Scholten, Everyday Leader

"*Secrets of Everyday Leaders* provides timeless wisdom for developing the people in your care. It's practical, inspiring, and will encourage anyone to step up and into purposeful 21st century living."

Paula Stern, Everyday Leader

"It's life-changing to discover that God uses ordinary people in extraordinary ways. That means you and me! *Secrets of Everyday Leaders* helps you discover hope, purpose, and fulfillment—cheering you on and supporting you as you become a biblically-trained servant leader."

Donna Burns, Everyday Leader

"*Secrets of Everyday Leaders* is a practical guide on leadership qualities and how to acquire them and put them into action. Jeff Myers has given me a desire to learn how to communicate, and to communicate well, which in turn is freeing me to become all that God has made me to be. His curriculum programs prove that leadership can be learned—everyone has the potential to become a leader if they are willing to learn."

Ned Ryun, Everyday Leader